Communications in Computer and Information Science   **813**

Commenced Publication in 2007
Founding and Former Series Editors:
Alfredo Cuzzocrea, Xiaoyong Du, Orhun Kara, Ting Liu, Dominik Ślęzak,
and Xiaokang Yang

More information about this series at http://www.springer.com/series/7899

María José Abásolo · Jorge Abreu
Pedro Almeida · Telmo Silva (Eds.)

Applications and Usability of Interactive Television

6th Iberoamerican Conference, jAUTI 2017
Aveiro, Portugal, October 12–13, 2017
Revised Selected Papers

Springer

Editors
María José Abásolo
CICPBA - III-LIDI
National University of La Plata
La Plata
Argentina

Jorge Abreu
University of Aveiro
Aveiro
Portugal

Pedro Almeida
University of Aveiro
Aveiro
Portugal

Telmo Silva
University of Aveiro
Aveiro
Portugal

ISSN 1865-0929   ISSN 1865-0937 (electronic)
Communications in Computer and Information Science
ISBN 978-3-319-90169-5   ISBN 978-3-319-90170-1   (eBook)
https://doi.org/10.1007/978-3-319-90170-1

Library of Congress Control Number: 2018940149

Printed on acid-free paper

This Springer imprint is published by the registered company Springer International Publishing AG part of Springer Nature
The registered company address is: Gewerbestrasse 11, 6330 Cham, Switzerland

Preface

The 6th Iberoamerican Conference on Applications and Usability of Interactive TV (jAUTI 2017) was held during October 12–13, 2017, in Aveiro (Portugal), and was organized by the Social iTV group of the DigiMedia Research Unit of the Universidade de Aveiro.

jAUTI 2017 was the sixth edition of a scientific event promoted by the RedAUTI Thematic Network on Applications and Usability of Interactive Digital Television. RedAUTI currently consists of more than 200 researchers from 32 universities and industry from Spain, Portugal, and 11 Latin American countries (Argentina, Brazil, Colombia, Costa Rica, Cuba, Chile, Ecuador, Guatemala, Perú, Uruguay, Venezuela).

These proceedings contain a collection of extended selected papers originally presented at jAUTI 2017, and later peer reviewed, that cover the development and deployment of technologies related to interactive digital TV, second screen applications, interfaces for TV, audiovisual content production and user experience studies of TV-related services and applications.

January 2018

María José Abásolo
Jorge Abreu
Pedro Almeida
Telmo Silva

Organization

Program Chairs

Jorge Abreu — University of Aveiro, Portugal
María José Abásolo — CICPBA/III-LIDI, National University of La Plata, Argentina
Pedro Almeida — University of Aveiro, Portugal
Telmo Silva — University of Aveiro, Portugal

Program Committee

Freddy Acosta — University of the Armed Forces ESPE, Ecuador
José Luis Arciniegas-Herrera — University of Cauca, Colombia
Sandra Baldassarri — University of Zaragoza, Spain
Valdecir Becker — Federal University of Paraíba, Brazil
Antoni Bibiloni — University of the Balearic Islands, Spain
Fernando Boronat — Polytechnic University of Valencia, Spain
Teresa Chambel — University of Lisboa, Portugal
Konstantinos Chorianopoulos — Ionian University, Greece
Cesar Collazos — University of Cauca, Colombia
Armando De Giusti — III-LIDI, National University of La Plata, Argentina
Sergi Fernandez-Langa — i2CAT Foundation, Spain
Angel García-Crespo — University Carlos III of Madrid, Spain
David Geerts — University of Leuven, Belgium
Israel Gonzalez-Carrasco — University Carlos III of Madrid, Spain
Roberto Guerrero — National University of San Luis, Argentina
Anelise Jantsch — Federal University of Rio Grande do Sul, Brazil
Rita Oliveira — University of Aveiro, Portugal
Patricia Oliveira — University of Aveiro, Portugal
Emili Prado — Autonomous University of Barcelona, Spain
Miguel Angel Rodrigo-Alonso — University of Córdoba, Spain
Josemar Rodrigues de Souza — University of the State of Bahia, Brazil
Cecilia Sanz — III LIDI, National University of La Plata, Argentina
Juan Carlos Torres — Technical University of Loja, Ecuador

Contents

IDTV Interaction Techniques and Accessibility

Invited Talk

Mobile Devices, a Complement to Television. Case Studies

Angel García-Crespo[1]([⊠]) , Inés García-Encabo[1], Carlos A. Matheus-Chacin[1], and María V. Diaz[2]

[1] Universidad Carlos III de Madrid, Avda Universidad 30, 28911 Leganés, Spain
angel.garcia@uc3m.es
[2] Universidad de Alcalá, C/Trinidad nº 5, 28801 Alcalá de Henares, Spain

Abstract. Today, television is not just a device; with new mobile devices, smartphones and tablets, together with the advent of streaming video platforms, the concept of television is an entire ecosystem in which all the elements of HW, SW and broadcast channels intermingle to provide a new version of entertainment. This article will review real cases of how mobile devices can become part of this new ecosystem. It presents a set of applications that enhance the television ecosystem through mobile apps, using the possibilities of smartphones and tablets to increase capacities from a user's point of view and that of the TV chains.

Keywords: Mobile device · Television · Sensory disabilities

1 Context

In 2007, Apple launched its first iPhone with iOs, and in late 2009, the first Android phones were released. Today these are the standards of the personal connectivity market. According to [6] at the end of 2015, the penetration of mobile phones in the world rose to 97%, and the number of mobile devices globally reached 7.9 billion, more than people on our planet. In Europe, 78 out of every 100 inhabitants have a smartphone. Global mobile traffic is predicted to grow by about 8 times between 2015 and 2020. By 2019, mobile video will account for 72% of all global mobile data traffic.

1.1 History. Mobile Devices for Access to Culture

Theater
More than 5% of the population suffers from a sensory disability (auditory or visual). In order to achieve equality in the total integration of people with disabilities [12], it is necessary to provide elements of accessibility to cultural events. For this purpose, techniques such as stenotyping, sign language interpretation or live audio-description have been used [7]. However, the foregoing are too expensive and depend on the availability of an expert at the time of the event. In 2011, the first experience of using smartphones for accessing cultural events, the UC3MTitling system for theatre, was presented [4]. The system allows both captions and the audio description, with two different modules.

M. J. Abásolo et al. (Eds.): jAUTI 2017, CCIS 813, pp. 3–14, 2018.
https://doi.org/10.1007/978-3-319-90170-1_1

The script editor, which uses the performance script in Word format, defines the styles for each of the characters in order to identify them correctly. This identification of the different characters is carried out by means of font, size, color and other text parameters, creating styles that are applied to all the text of that character, allowing subtitles to bring an unlimited number of styles.

Once the script has been generated in the first module, the system creates a file that is used to display the titles of a VGA or HDMI output from a computer or sent over the internet on devices such as tablets or smartphones, as shown in Fig. 1.

This was a first step in bringing culture closer to people with disabilities through a smartphone and integrating these devices as an expanded screen of the world.

Films

In September 2013, the WhatsCine system was introduced, which makes cinema accessible, enabling blind people to listen to the audiodescription of the film without interfering with the audio of other viewers. At the same time, it allows the deaf to watch sign language through special glasses or follow the subtitling, all through their smartphone. As it is a multi-language application, captions in any language are available.

WhatsCine operates within a local wireless network that provides coverage to anyone who wants to make use of accessibility. A computer is connected to this wireless network and functions as a server. This server is the main component of the system as it contains the software necessary to manage the audio description. It is also houses the videos with the sign language and the files needed to play the subtitles. Likewise, it manages synchronization with viewers to indicate when the playback is taking place and to show everyone the same content simultaneously, as can be seen in Fig. 2.

Fig. 1. Different devices in which it is possible to view the subtitles transmitted over the internet

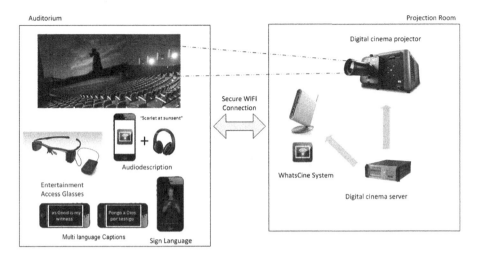

Fig. 2. Whatscine system initial architecture

Each viewer connects to the accessibility server via their personal mobile device. These terminals receive audio from the audio description, the video with the sign language and the content of the subtitles, all in a synchronized fashion, through the wireless network. The advantage of client terminals is that it is the users' own intelligent devices (smartphones and tablets) that are used to receive accessibility elements, making implementation of the WhatsCine system even more viable (WhatsCine has been developed for iOS and Android mobile platforms.)

The three main functionalities the system offers are visibly differentiated and separated within the application. They are easily accessible to all people as they are properly labeled so that the accessibility assistants of the terminals themselves can find them. In the case of a blind individual who wishes to enter the audiodescription, they can simply scroll with their finger on the screen of the device so that it tells them what option they are using and confirm with a double click where they wish to enter.

Of course, not all accessibility methods may be required for all events, so if only the audio description and subtitling option are set up on the server for example, the sign language feature will not be visible on the terminals.

Audiodescription

Audiodescription basically consists of providing sound information on all those data, situations and details that are essential for understanding of certain cultural acts and events that only appear visually [13]. It also allows audio description to be received without the need for a special device (such as a frequency modulated receiver), enabling the audio description to be heard from the personal device of the viewer, without interfering with the audio for the rest of the room.

Subtítles (captions)

The purpose of subtitles is to show the dialogues, translated or not, of a scene in a movie or play, along with relevant information that can indicate the sounds produced in the

Fig. 3. Sign language interpreter on a smartphone

scene. The characteristic feature of the subtitles is that they can be used not only to help hearing impaired people follow a play or film, but also for situations where further information needs to be presented in addition to the visual or when it is necessary to show actors' conversations or a speaker's speech in a language other than the one that they speak. Like the audio description, captioning is also set up in the interface of the server software. In this interface, one must specify the files that contain the subtitles along with the name that appears in the client application interface.

An important aspect to keep in mind about subtitles is the format in which they must be stored on the server and properly displayed in client applications. The applications, both in iOS and Android, read these files and are displayed on the device at the pace indicated by the server. The subtitles are contained in XML files according to the Digital Cinema Package (DCP) projection standard [2]. DCP stands for the archive or set of compressed and encrypted files that encompasses the content and associated information of a movie or short film.

The user selects a subtitle language that corresponds to a file stored on the server. The client applications will be in charge of reading this file, interpreting it, asking the server at what time of the session it is and carrying a timer that displays the subtitles read as time goes by. The viewer's application periodically checks with the server the time of the event and checks that the subtitles are being displayed properly in order to avoid synchronization errors that can be bothersome and cause difficulties in understanding.

Sign Language

Sign language is the last accessibility option offered in the system and is also aimed at those users with hearing disabilities who prefer sign language to subtitles.

In the same way that we proceed with the subtitles, we proceed with the videos of sign language. The video file is accessed from the viewer's application and the server is asked the time in seconds from the beginning of the session to adjust the playback to the moment it occurs. Playback will then continue uninterruptedly until the user desires.

The only thing that appears on the device screen is the video with the interpreter as shown in Fig. 3.

1.2 Results

Mobile devices provide a solution for the accessibility and integration of people with sensory disabilities into society and culture. Because they are based on personal mobile devices, the need for more complex technical alternatives is avoided, taking advantage of the widespread use of smartphones and tablets.

2 Accessibility in Television via Mobile Devices

Based on the systems explained above, an audio detection algorithm is incorporated into the applications to synchronize with audiovisual material, incorporating accessibility not only for cinema, but also for television. One of the problems with VoD (Video On Demand) platforms is precisely the inclusion of accessibility elements. While in many countries, accessibility elements are not mandatory by law, it should be a moral obligation. In the USA, the Americans with Disabilities Act [9] requires new audiovisual content published on the Internet to have closed captioning.

The inclusion of closed captions only covers part of the population with sensory disabilities, leaving the blind out completely because of not including audio description. It also fails to meet the needs of a significant part of the deaf population, who need sign language for optimal communication.

Given the possibilities of WhatsCine to make audiovisual content accessible with audio synchronization technology, a new app is being developed that enables synchronization with a VoD television, in this case Movistar+ [3]. Since August 2015, the Movistar + platform has been offering film in an accessible format through audio synchronism technology without any additional cost.

The hearing-impaired can choose between Spanish Sign Language (LSE) and subtitles, which offers, in addition to the transcription of dialogues, identification of characters by means of colors, information on sounds and the intonation of dialogues. Neither the LSE interpreter and subtitles invade the TV screen but rather are displayed on the smartphone screen or the user's tablet.

Similarly, the visually-impaired can use the audio-description system, which works through headphones connected to the smartphone or tablet.

The system designed for television accessibility consists of an app that contains a repository with the accessibility elements of the films or series of the VoD

Fig. 4. Two lecterns simultaneously displaying the two-language subtitles of a television program

platform. The viewer chooses the accessibility element (adapted subtitles, sign language to audio-description) of the audiovisual material they want to use and the system synchronizes the material from the audio. This synchronization is done on an internal server to which a few seconds of audio captured by the device of the viewer are sent and this server returns the time where the audiovisual material is found.

This system thereby provides a solution for the accessibility and integration of people with sensory disabilities, and as it is based on personal mobile devices, it avoids the need for more complex technical alternatives, taking advantage of the widespread use of smartphones and tablets.

It is true that it may be a nuisance for the spectator who wishes to watch the subtitles or sign language on his or her device and on television, and for this purpose an augmented reality system has been designed so that the hearing impaired can enjoy the accessibility elements more freely. A special lectern has been patented that allows both the subtitles and the sign language to be viewed at the same time as the audiovisual elements in an environment of augmented reality (Figs. 4 and 5).

3   Interconnection with Other Devices

Deafblindness is a combination of low vision and hearing loss, not necessarily complete deafness and complete blindness. Deafblind people have unique challenges in the areas of mobility and communication. It is a unique and diverse disability due to the wide range of sensory abilities, the presence of additional disabilities and the age of onset. A deaf-blind person faces unique difficulties in interacting with the world around him/her.

To do this, a system was designed that from the subtitles that are broadcast in the different channels of TDT in format (DVB-TXT) and with a mobile application will send these subtitles to an app that will communicate with a Braille line.

In Spain, and in other countries, free DTT channels have the legal obligation to broadcast a large number of subtitled programmes. These subtitles can be picked up from the broadcast transport stream and sent to viewers' devices to be read by voice synthesis or a Braille line so that deaf-blind people can access them.

The system that was developed has the following basic functionalities:

Subtitle extraction module. This module allows the extraction and processing of subtitles (DVB-TXT) collected from the free-to-air broadcast of the DTT channel.

Subtitle Display Management Module. This module will allow the visualization of subtitles extracted by the previous system in the devices of the spectators (ANDROID and iOS).

These developed modules will allow the multiple interaction of users and chains.

The system is currently implemented for all the national and regional channels in the Community of Madrid, which is where the extractor is housed, to which the DTT signal for each multiplex is connected.

Although in principle only the realization of a DVB-TXT subtitle extractor was planned, DVB-SUB subtitles are also extracted, not as text but as an image and an OCR text recognition process is carried out to convert them into text and send them to the central server.

Two GoAll apps have also been developed, one for Android and the other for iOS that allow connection with Braille lines and configuration of the subtitle broadcast.

Fig. 5. Lectern in a cinema showing a sign language interpreter and simultaneous subtitling

In Fig. 6, the main menu of the app is shown where you choose the string from which you want to view the subtitles or send to the Braille line (Figs. 7, 8, 9 and 10).

Fig. 6. TV subtitle viewing module input screen

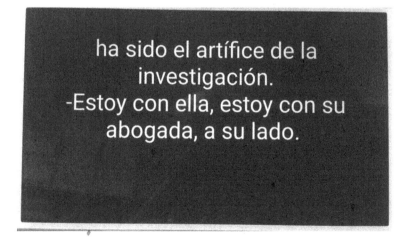

Fig. 7. Real-time subtitle display

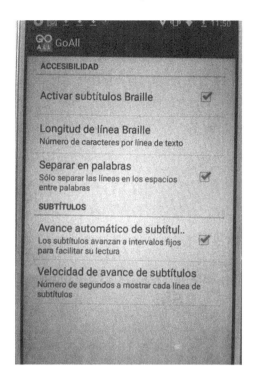

Fig. 8. Accessibility options for connection to the Braille line

Fig. 9. Blind person using the system

Fig. 10. The system running on the Braille line

4   New Possibilities, Mobile Devices as Hearing Aids

Modern hearing aids have improved a lot compared to the technology available only 20 years ago, but they still have a long way to go to serve the approximately 360 million people in the world who have low hearing [5]. Many people with severe hearing loss can understand speech quite well if the sound comes directly to a hearing device eliminating noise and improving some aspects of sound, but today's hearing instruments have certain limitations such as there is no easy way to connect them wirelessly and reliably to the full range of audio technologies needed today.

Today a smarphone contains all the components needed to build a personal hearing aid. It contains a microphone, a loudspeaker and, in the middle, all the necessary processing power. Right now there are some applications (apps) that amplify sound, but this not only improves hearing abilities, because people who have a hearing deficit also need to modify certain characteristics of sound, and this modification is different for each person.

An app is being designed to allow a customized configuration so that each user can adjust the different frequencies that make up the sound to suit their needs, since hearing loss is usually the loss of sensitivity in some, but not all frequencies, being this the operation of a conventional hearing aid, amplify some frequencies more than others, this allows people with hearing loss and not using a hearing aid can access the sound of television.

This is important because hearing loss is often associated with intolerance to loud sounds and noisy environments, such as a common workroom or a multiple meeting. It may seem strange that a hearing aid should make some sounds quieter, but in this way you can get the hearing-impaired person to hear again.

Hearing aids are associated with improved communication and quality of life, but often unaffordable or inaccessible to many adults. The high cost (~400€ for a hearing aid) and inconvenience (multiple visits needed for installation and adjustments) limit access for many adults.

Hearing loss in older adults is highly prevalent and doubles every decade, beginning at age 40 [8]. Age-related hearing loss begins gradually and may progress for years before an individual begins to experience subjective hearing difficulties [1]. In addition, hearing disorders tend to initially manifest themselves in difficult listening situations, such as working group discussions or conversations in a noisy environment, such as a restaurant. The gradual progression and common occurrence of age-related hearing loss leads many people to communication difficulties [11].

Less than 20% of people with hearing loss use hearing aids, which highlights the need for new approaches to the provision of listening technologies and services to reduce the gap between those with hearing loss and those who are able and willing to access care.

According to the study carried out by [10] "Personal Sound Amplifiers for Adults with Hearing Loss" the main hearing devices recommended for the direct consumer and their main technological and user characteristics, where the market leaders are evaluated: Bean T-Coil, CS-50+, Tweak Focus, Soundhawk and Songbird all have a price above 250 dollars".

The main innovation of the project being developed: AudiSmart, is to make a hearing impaired person's hearing aid available on their own smartphone, not limited to a general amplification of the sound, but through specifically designed algorithms, as background noise increases, the gain is gradually reduced to keep production at a manageable level. After all, when the background is noisy, soft, loud sounds are masked, and the amplification only serves to make the noise more annoying. A high gain does not offer benefits in noisy situations. The system will effectively and customize the audio signal to suit the particular needs of each individual.

AudiSmart is not intended to be a simple sound amplifier, it will be a sound amplifier application, the experience of the SoftLab research group in sound processing as well as the experience that has allowed it to develop and evaluate systems such as UC3Mtitling, WhatsCine or GoAll, have allowed it to develop and evaluate a pre/processing algorithm for acoustic stimuli. It is important to think of AudiSmart as the app-based implementation of an algorithm.

5   Conclusions

The use of mobile devices and the internet has enabled us to develop all these technologies as free end user apps without any cost for the disabled individual.

The actions carried out in the SoftLab research group since 2006, when work began to promote accessibility for people with sensory disabilities. Have been marked by the awareness and development of systems that allow access to culture and education for people with sensory disabilities in all aspects. The latest project under development for the collective of deafblind people is noteworthy, as it has always been the maxim of the research group that although the number of people who with a disability is minimal, we must always find a solution so that they can have to culture.

As can be seen, all of the progress made in audiovisual accessibility has been come about by seeking to create viable and useful systems for people with disabilities, such as those presented in this article, all of which are in operation.

Acknowledgements. The Pervasive technology was supported by Telefonica and the AudiSmart technology is supported by INDRA and Fundación Universia.

References

1. Basic facts about hearing loss. http://www.hearingloss.org/content/basic-facts-about-hearing-loss
2. Digital cinema system specification, v.1.2. http://www.dcimovies.com/archives/spec_v1_2_No_Errata_Incorporated/DCIDigitalCinemaSystemSpecv1_2.pdf
3. García-Crespo, Á., López-Cuadrado, J.L., González-Carrasco, I.: Accesibilidad en plataformas de VoD mediante plataformas móviles: piloto en Movistar. In: VI International Conference on Interactive Digital TV IV Iberoamerican Conference on Applications and Usability of Interactive TV, p. 115 (2015)
4. García-Crespo, A., González-Carrasco, I., López-Cuadrado, J.L., Ruiz-Mezcua, B.: Herramienta Interactiva para la Realización de la Accesibilidad a Eventos en Directo. In: Libro de actas DRT4ALL 2011 IV Congreso Internacional de Diseño, Redes de Investigación y Tecnología para todos, pp. 501–507 (2011)
5. Houtenville, A.J., Erickson, W.A., Lee, C.G.: Disability statistics from the American Community Survey (ACS). Cornell University Rehabilitation Research and Training Center on Disability Demographics and Statistics, Ithaca (2007)
6. Informe Mobile en España y en el Mundo 2016. http://www.amic.media/media/files/file_352_1050.pdf
7. Cintas, J.D.: La accesibilidad a los medios de comunicación audiovisual a través del subtitulado y la audiodescripción. Cooperación y Diálogo, p. 157 (2010)
8. Lengnick-Hall, M.L., Gaunt, P.M., Kulkarni, M.: Overlooked and underutilized: people with disabilities are an untapped human resource. Hum. Resour. Manage. **47**(2), 255–273 (2008)
9. Lips, B.W.: The Americans with disabilities act of 1990 (1993)
10. Mamo, S.K., Reed, N.S., Nieman, C.L., Oh, E.S., Lin, F.R.: Personal sound amplifiers for adults with hearing loss. Am. J. Med. **129**(3), 245–250 (2016)
11. National institute on deafness and other communication disorders (NIDCD): quick statistics about hearing (2016). www.nidcd.nih.gov/health/statistics/quick-statisticshearing
12. Organización de las Naciones Unidas. Convención sobre los derechos de las personas con discapacidad. http://www.un.org/esa/socdev/enable/documents/tccconvs.pdf. Última visita 15 May 2013
13. UNE 153020: Audiodescripción para personas con discapacidad visual: requisitos para la audiodescripción y elaboración de audioguías. AENOR, Madrid (2005)

Design and Evaluation of IDTV Services and Content

Audiovisual Design: Introducing 'Media Affordances' as a Relevant Concept for the Development of a New Communication Model

Valdecir Becker[1] , Daniel Gambaro[2](✉) , Thais Saraiva Ramos[3] ,
and Rafael Moura Toscano[1]

[1] Postgraduate Program in Computer Science,
Communication and Arts (PPGCCA), Informatics Centre,
Federal University of Paraiba, João Pessoa, Brazil
[2] Postgraduate Program in Audiovisual Media and Processes,
School of Communications and Arts (PPGMPA),
University of São Paulo, São Paulo, Brazil
dgambaro@usp.br
[3] Audiovisual Design Research Group, CNPq, Brasília, Brazil
audiovisualdesign@lavid.ufpb.br

Abstract. Audiovisual Design is a communication model, represented by a methodology of analysis and development of content that mixes audiovisual elements with interaction software and digital interfaces. This essay introduces the concept of media affordances in Audiovisual Design as a contribution to understanding and planning of actions taken by a person during production and enjoyment of sound and video using the contemporary set of media. The model represents the intersection between Human-Computer Interaction Studies and Media Studies, required to develop audiovisual and sound content today. The present text introduces definitions of Audiovisual Design and outlines the concept of affordances, characteristics of mediatic tools required for an individual to perform an assigned role, or step from one to another. This involves processes of learning and assimilating available affordances in different contexts. Audiovisual producers must be able to understand and predict how Audience, in different levels of engagement or inertia, will react in face of tools available through content and interfaces of distribution.

Keywords: Audiovisual Design · Human-Computer Interaction
Media Studies · Affordances

1 Introduction

The communicational-methodological model of Audiovisual Design (AD) reunites methods and concepts from two traditionally isolated fields that share similar approaches: Human-Computer Interaction, from Computer Sciences, and Media Studies, from Communication Sciences. To give a brief description, AD shows two practical features: (1) To analyse audiovisual content produced with tools from both HCI and Media Studies altogether; (2) To predict user interactions and propose

© Springer International Publishing AG, part of Springer Nature 2018
M. J. Abásolo et al. (Eds.): jAUTI 2017, CCIS 813, pp. 17–31, 2018.
https://doi.org/10.1007/978-3-319-90170-1_2

innovative applications of those tools in development of audiovisual creations. The model's main characteristic is the planning of interaction – or interactivity – simultaneously with creation and production of audio and/or video features, which occurs based upon four *Lines of Design* that configure and shape the creative process: Identity, Motivations, Experience and Content [1].

The integration of those elements (interactive tools and content) has altered the creation and production processes. The design and development of audiovisual content, including applications that make use of video, is swiftly changing in response to technological convergence. Individually, HCI and Media Studies do not contemplate changes in these two fields. The design of interactive computational systems initially focused on problem solving, tasks and functions; later, its reach was slowly broadened to incorporate other perspectives, such as novel possibilities, significances and emotions; and now people's behaviour is also contemplated. For instance, passive enjoyment gains relevance when the final object of the interactive system is an audiovisual content.

The same phenomenon is observable through the audiovisual consumption's perspective, once software usage has become as relevant as the quality of movies, TV series, online videos and sound content. All digital media for accessing content show a similar characteristic: interaction through software. The spectator's experience mixes an active posture (navigation and search for information) with moments of passive fruition (visualisation of content) in tasks such as accessing digital TV schedule guide, searching for a title in applications as Netflix, or recommending a video or audio content through social media. In other words, the simple act of choosing and watching a video programme may require the individual to assume different roles, with higher or lower levels of interaction and participation. Consequently, a revision of theories and methods supporting content development becomes necessary, especially in HCI field, in which the notion of 'users' has a limited part by not contemplating their total immersion in different media, especially audiovisual ones.

To adequately respond to this new scenario of audiovisual content production and fruition, in which audio, video and software are integrated in a single workpiece, AD defines four roles a person can assume: Audience, Synthesiser, Modifier, and Producer [1]. Uses of available resources afforded in each performed role vary in degrees of engagement and inertia.

The distinction of a set of actions – or interactions – made possible by various technologies in different moments of audiovisual consumption is a key element to understand alterations in level of actions related to storytelling or content – which, subsequently, may cause individuals to step from one role to another. In this essay, we are introducing the concept of *affordances* in the AD model. In short, the concept refers to potential uses an object may have and how such attributes allow users to carry out an action. For Norman [2], affordances must be conventional and consistent, a design principle emphasising the need for explicit cues that demonstrate to users what they can do with a device/system. Design must provide sufficient information/suggestions of 'what can be done' and how people should interact with the tool. Since users need some motivation to act, without desire or drive to seek out possible uses they are likely to overlook them or simply fail in action.

AD considers that individuals, to alternate between roles, must understand the set of available actions (those the Producer expects they will undertake or avoid), as well as how they can subvert the medium to their own advantage or according to their own welfares. It is an essential concept in the convergence between theories and methods from HCI and Media Studies, where software becomes central to content enjoyment, whether through digital TV, internet or on-demand services of audio and video.

The article has the following structure: the AD model is presented in Sect. 2; Sect. 3 holds the conceptualization of affordance and its pertinence to media studies, while Sect. 4 presents elements regarding learning of affordances. Section 5 closes this essay by presenting some conclusions regarding application of model, and features that require further investigation.

2 The Audiovisual Design Communication Model

The communication processes can be defined using theoretical and conceptual models, describing communicative acts and the flow of information among people and present and acting communication technologies [3]. Recently, new models have been suggested, aiming to understand how the notion of individuality – and communities created around the generalisation of the concept – impact on media and on content creation. Jenkins et al. [4] proposed three simple models to describe different current communication scenarios: from one communicator to multiple recipients, Broadcast; online communication in which individuals have initiative of searching content, as Stickiness; and Spreadable, when content reaches an audience through actions of persons, mostly using digital tools. The authors describe the communication processes as connected to exchange of information and to various modes of media consumption.

However, Jenkins et al. [4] did not contemplate the technical-creative process of audiovisual production, where the subjectiveness of storytelling links to the objectiveness of interaction requirement. Interface problems, or bad user experiences, may compromise the entire audiovisual product. Some of those elements can be approached by technological learning and identification of possibilities of use of communication interfaces. In contrast, these matters are broadly studied by HCI. While audiovisual fruition has been hitherto considered a simple process with no requirements for technological mastery, software development rests upon the capability of use by individuals, that is, potentialities of action regarding the perception one holds towards an object or a technology when interacting with it [5].

In contemporaneity, increased presence of technology in different daily situations (mediatisation) profoundly transforms the media ecosystem. Besides the emergence of new technologies, complementarity between existing means is extended, and they combine themselves in different communication processes [6]. Such transformations have some impact in people's lives by bringing new possibilities of use and interaction, through the properties of each technology individually and convergences among those technologies. AD contributes to understand these arrangements, pointing that separate affordances of a technology applied in the production and distribution of content, as well as competencies required to its use, are essential to the existence of multiple roles an individual (or person, or user) can assume.

2.1 Audiovisual Design

From the context outlined above, previous studies [1] identified the need of a theoretical and methodological model to integrate software development and audiovisual content creation. The Audiovisual Design results from the intersection of HCI and Media Studies. It is represented by a graphic workflow that allows recognition of the dynamic flow of audiovisual production considering a variety of scenarios and roles performed by individuals (Fig. 1) [1].

Although dominant in software development processes, 'user' is typically an abstract individual commonly identified by archetypes. Instead, in the AD model one person can perform different roles in different moments: Audience, Synthesiser, Modifier, and Producer.

Audience: this is the basis for all roles an individual can assume; it denotes low level or absence of interaction during media consumption. It is the passive behaviour associated to the Broadcast model, approaching digital interfaces through selection of channels, search and playing of content, subscription to a feed or channel, etc. Hence those people are identified in groups by audience ratings or data about access to a given content,

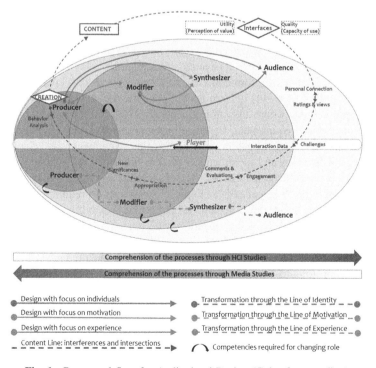

Fig. 1. Processual flow for Audiovisual Design (Color figure online)

enabling only a collective vision of their preferences. The relationship of individuals with content occurs in the level of personal taste and remains relatively private.

Synthesiser: the concept was brought in by Jenkins, Ford and Green from an idea developed by Bradley Horowitz [4]. These individuals present competencies to compile, classify, comment, recommend and share content they like, usually to construct a digital 'identity', a staged profile in a social network. Synthesiser's role considers the notion of engagement, the emotional link that allows people to express something about themselves using content to which they relate.

Modifier: this is the group of individuals that appropriate and transform content to express something about themselves. These super-engaged hardcore fans shall acquire competences to perform this role. There are a set of activities that determines if one belongs to this role: *remixing*, that is, appropriation of content to create something new, connected or not to the original idea; *improvement*, or modifying the original content to amend something one dislikes about it, altering the original meaning or result of a narrative; *participation*, when the person interacts with and transforms the show (live or recorded) while it is being produced, thus altering the output and becoming a temporary co-producer.

Producer: a person or group of people who creates original content (even if inspired by other media content); they can either be autonomous and independent or collaborators in great media corporations. Every Producer is a Synthesiser by nature because he or she holds competencies for content distribution, but the competencies of the Modifier only apply when industrially-crafted content is an adaptation of another, existing one. For this reason, the superposition of both roles is only partially represented in the figure.

Player: is not a role, but an 'enhancement' within each role. The term refers to individuals who fully use the tools available for and in each level, becoming Player-Audience, Player-Synthesiser, Player-Modifier and Player-Producer. Their actions, especially those not foreseen in the design of the workpiece, shall feed the Producer in future developments. In other words, Players can perceive and learn affordances not foreseen to their level. Players pursue challenging content that makes them, even if individually, think and perform an action. One may identify them (not restrictively) with 'early adopters' or 'early users', that is, those who will assume the risk of using a new technology and, thus, contribute to its development. The AD model tries to predict every user behaviour, but it would be a mistake not to consider unpredicted uses.

Finally, the two arrows at the graphic's bottom represent how the process is comprehended within Media Studies and HCI Studies. The blue arrow refers to the relationship of people with the content, that is, objectives, intentions and meanings implied in (and derived from) enjoying the audiovisual programme. Diverse intellectual traditions are usually combined in such an approach, for instance Cultural Studies, Semiology and Ethnography. It is emphasised how discourses are interpreted and incorporated by people, which may lead to a understanding of the creative process itself. In other words, through Media Studies one starts with a general context to try and understand Producer's motivations – whether economic, cultural or ideological – and so point out his or her intentions. The main advantage in analysing the process of audiovisual creation using this perspective is to come to acknowledge sociocultural concerns in a given local or historical context, plus how such concerns exert influence (or even determine) choices made by the Producer. Data collected from observation of the relationship of public with programme output are then feedbacked to the audiovisual industry's production chain, apart from becoming the basis for creation of policies designed to cultural development.

Nonetheless, even if the content (format, theme and storytelling) is the foundation of the creative process of an audiovisual product, to consider interactions performed by audience through different interfaces requires the Producer to also contemplate processes and technical and technological courses that will lead to the content.

HCI presents methods and processes that help composing such perspective. The fruition process is divided into steps, planned in accordance to possible engagement an individual will demonstrate regarding enjoyment of the programme and motivation to contribute to the richness of content. This field of studies enables planning and comprehension of the production process of an audiovisual piece by looking at all elements parallel to the content, usually sprang from the technologies employed for enjoyment. That is how the concept of *affordances* becomes necessary. Starting from the production sphere and continuing in the direction of the most passive audience, the HCI axis (purple arrow) allows to underline different demands for a workpiece, by considering its format and technology employed and the more active or less active utilisation individuals will do of possibilities offered in a technological context. For example, a programme that includes a complex interactional system, to be developed for the parcel of audience showing a major engagement level, requires a detailed planning based upon: problem identification, creation of scenarios, survey with selected people, analysis of gathered data, continuous and self-fed planning of usage methodologies (incorporating feedback coming from surveys and first uses), directly applied to development of the audiovisual workpiece. The phase of problem identification is also the phase of documentation of *affordances* of each technological support in which the content will be available. Hence scenarios should be created considering different levels of activity (from most active to most passive) and the selection of technologies (including in production sphere) that may impact in how the content will be perceived by each person.

Thus, the encounter of both theoretical fields helps to explain platforms of work and of circulation, themes and possible spread of audience in each environment and platform delimited by the Producer. On its turn, the act of delimitation is informed by data arisen from the creation process (HCI axis) and data referring social and cultural uses and appropriations (Media Studies).

3 Affordances

As shown in the description of the AD workflow, how the designer or producer aim his or her workpiece to reach different levels of AD-assigned roles, and how they are related among themselves, rely upon the content, the technics and the interfaces that fulfil objectives individually defined by each person. Those objectives correspond directly to the way people get involved with a production (privately or publicly, passively or actively, as spectator or as co-producer). This requires individuals to bare a 'set of *competencies*' – a concept that will be further explained later in this section – adequate to technological affordances made available by the audiovisual product and its interfaces.

Such conclusion comes from a discussion common to HCI studies, one that observes the best technology learning methods and the perception of resources available in or offered by digital technologies. It is a practicality that good designs, whichever of products, interfaces or systems, must be intuitive, with reduced mental load to users [2, 7], inside technological and intellectual limits and the narrative's aims. Thus, it is pursued a fast, automatic comprehension of resources in each interaction artefact or device. Inside HCI, this discussion is centred around the concept of '*affordance*'.

The term comes from ecological psychology, proposed by Gibson [8, 9] to explain possibilities of action offered by an environment to a given actor. The author developed a theory of perception applied to every animal, including human beings. According to him, animals can perceive how much they can use of and interact with the environment. Available signals that can be recognised by animals are called 'affordances'. Hence Gibson came to conclude that affordances are physical properties of the environment, meaning they can be objectively measured and studied, as well as information available for perception. 'The central question for the theory of affordances is not whether they exist and are real but whether information is available in ambient light for perceiving them' [9, p. 132]. Affordances do not automatically present themselves to actors but must be uncovered through perception and learning. This process '…may require much exploration, patience, and time' [10, p. 17].

Three main constraints can shape affordances: (1) 'Logical constraints' are limitations imposed on the user by rules of action, inherent to every interaction; (2) 'Cultural constraints' are 'learned conventions that are shared by a cultural group', and may be understood as learned behaviours; and (3) 'Physical constraints' are fixed parameters of every interface that can be used to help user's achievement [2].

Norman [2] expanded this line of thought to design, explaining how important is to keep products with a simple and intuitive design to use and learning. The author agrees that affordance is a characteristic of the object, and it rests upon the person to notice it to interact with (or to adequately use). However, to Norman (as well as to Gibson) an affordance does not depend on personal perception to exist, it remains latent until it is necessary in a context. The author says an essential part of intuitive design refers to perception. It is not enough a good design be rational and logical. Excellent and intuitive designs are those that allow one to see, directly and correctly, what is possible to do with the designed thing.

Other authors, however, noticed that good and correct use of complex systems required more than mere existence of *interaction triggers*. Affordance is then, when one considers human interaction, a relative feature of the environment dependent on the individual's perception, which includes previous knowledge, social insertion, cultural aspects, etc. Thus, affordances may vary circumstantially from person to person, being *real* (those accorded to the environment), *hidden* (not naturally revealed by perceptible properties, so for users to determine the existence of most affordances, further perceptual information must be added), *false* (erroneous indications of possibilities of interaction) and *perceived* (assimilated by the individual) [2].

From Norman's affordances to support users during an interaction, Hartson [11] proposed a classification into four types, reflecting users' processes and types of actions undertook when performing a task. Norman's *perceived affordance* can instead be named as *cognitive affordance*, helping users with their cognitive actions to identify tool's features (recognising what it is and what it is for). *Real affordance* turns into *physical affordance*, aiding users in their physical actions (e.g., pushing, pressing, rolling, etc.). Then we have *sensory affordance* playing an important role in design and evaluation of interaction, to assist users with their sensorial actions (e.g. size, colour, audibility and feel). The fourth type, *functional affordance*, refers to the purposeful action component of physical affordances, which themselves are perceptible and actionable properties of a thing, whether in real world or virtual/graphical ones. This affordance fits in with user-centred design approach, by determining and focusing on the individual's aims and objectives.

These four types of affordances can be mapped back to Norman's action model: the act of passing from an intention of interaction – or identification of opportunity – to planning a sequence of actions requires *cognitive* and *sensory affordances. Physical* and *sensory affordances* are related to execution of this sequence of actions: *sensory affordances* are associated with perception of the state of the world, while *cognitive affordances* are necessary to interpret the perception.

3.1   About Competencies

Before applying the concept of media affordances by the AD, it is necessary to make an introduction to the concept of *competencies*, that is, characteristics shown by individuals, whether innate or developed, that are required by the environment and objects' affordances to fulfil an action or a reaction.

Competency is a terminology common to various fields. For example, in Business Administration and Human Resources, it refers to behavioural repertoire and intentions of a person to efficiently perform a given task [12, 13]. This comprehension can be extrapolated beyond workplace, since people must show intention, action and behaviour in every intentionally-engaged interaction. A competency, that is, what makes possible to competently performing a task, involves knowledges, skills and capabilities of individuals, ordered according to behaviours and intentions [13, 14]. We identify as skills an individual's subsets of characteristics that allow him or her to perform an intentional operation. Skills are acquired and developed from the intention of a person to act or react to a situation, thus shaping his or her behaviour during action he or she is engaging with. Capabilities, on the other hand, are 'potential skills' present in subconscious level and not yet developed. Capabilities are inherent to learning processes, an intermediate stage between acquisition of knowledge and using a skill to perform an action or a reaction.

In face of new communicational affordances originated in contemporary media ecosystem, individuals are expected to show new competencies (new sets of skills, knowledge, capabilities and behaviours), or to develop those culturally and psychologically rooted.

Socioeconomic, cultural, technical or technological background may provide elements to compose competencies. AD considers them as related to physical-economic conditions for accessing content; act of fruition, cultural use and appropriation of the message transmitted during the communicative process; how such act of fruition, appropriation and use occurs; and knowledge on required technologies to undertake a giver use. A competency is only effective when skills, knowledges and behaviours are aligned and activate *affordances* of a technology of communication (a media affordance). Therefore, appropriation of theories or notions of operation are not enough to ensure that a person has really acquired the competencies to be categorised into any AD-assigned role. He or she must first incorporate that function during the enjoyment of the audiovisual workpiece. We may assert that the individual effectively moved in between roles only after the process is started. Consequently, there is an opening both for progression and regression of each person between roles, what can be exemplified through the Line of Identity: a person may use every tool available to engage more fully with a programme that touches him or her profoundly, and can be a mere passive spectator to another, with which he or she relate only for entertainment satisfaction. The competencies necessary to occupy an AD-assigned role varies according to production characteristics and how individuals interact. In addition, since one role is contained in another, competencies accumulate from one level to level.

The Audience role clearly requires the simplest and most easily appropriable competencies. For the viewer who only watch audiovisual content in Broadcast model, cultural and linguistic competencies for understanding and interpretation of the message are basically enough. However, when we think about the increasing number of individuals using alternative fruition forms to Broadcast, but still for passive consumption – such as on demand video – skills accumulate. Among the competencies of Synthesisers, we emphasize those related to social media. To create their network identities, Synthesisers are part of communities of mutual interests and act as representations of themselves, hence they become poles within social networks articulated by digital media. These competencies also make evident one's condition as a fan, whose discussions revolve around their active participation in available content activities.

Regarding the role of Modifier, appropriation of technology is fundamental, especially when Producers do not release tools for modification. The appropriation of content that occurs at this level is a cultural appropriation of some parts or of the whole workpiece or technology, including generation of meaning, sense or a different discourse from that originally manifested in the workpiece. The Modifier gets elements from original context, modifies them, or recreates parts to transform them in a representative idea, or even in an ideology. From a sociological point of view, it can represent a very aggressive capability of expression, especially when the group appropriating content is a minority that uses a popular resource to make itself heard. Modifiers can create their own social network, becoming important nodes of content diffusion.

Producers' competencies are more complex, divided mainly between the field of technology and the ability to interpret the users' demands. Except for a few authorial or amateur projects, an audiovisual production usually involves a group of people, thus each person who works at a project, shows his or her own competencies within the area of expertise. This is common in large commercial products (e.g. writers, system developers, editors, graphic designers). Even if a person cannot master all technologies involved in a production, it is important to be aware of which ones are present to provide a seamless user experience.

3.2   Media Affordances

In a wide perspective, according to AD first the Producer must develop *functional affordances* to incite individuals' interest and call attention to the programme. How other AD-assigned roles evaluate the content – whether it deserves audience, synthetisation or improvement – rely on adequate awareness of value, including subjective elements related to informational value or potential entertainment, and available resources of participation, interaction or sharing. Now, in a narrower perspective, analysis of content and of interaction are directly linked to individuals' level of activity. Alternation of roles depends on correct perception of *physical affordances*, which are associated to the environment and can be:

1. physical, those which can actively be manipulated and potential uses are perceptually obvious, composed by technologies used for content fruition, e.g. remote control, mouse, virtual keyboards, computer screens or TV sets. The environment is relevant because it conceals or reveals *physical affordances*, also impacting on *sensory* and *cognitive affordances*.
2. of interactional graphic interfaces, such as interactive TV menus or 'share buttons' in on-demand video systems. This has always been a paramount subject to development of interactive TV, since deficiency in digital culture (the impossibility of perception of *physical affordances*, consequently eliminating *cognitive* and *sensory* ones) derail the use of complex interaction interfaces by people without technological and relational knowledge of internet [15].
3. symbolic narrative, where *physical affordances* are subtler, and *cognitive* and *sensory affordances* rely not only on technology and interfaces, but also on comprehension of narrative elements. As example, cues and cliff-hangers from a character in a drama serial, aiming at action of one AD-assigned role, or calls to action of hosts in programmes, employing work of Synthesisers. In this case, *physical affordances* can be voice, a song, an image composing a scene, or a set of actualities that stimulates curiosity (that is, a *cognitive affordance*).

Depending on context, some affordances must be noticed only by individuals performing a given role, otherwise action may be prevented. Producers must establish several features (or perceptual cues) to help users recognise the correct affordances.

As for *sensory affordances*, they present two important functions. First, mediation and link between *physical* and *cognitive affordances*, which are necessary to identify the goal and associate it to a possible outcome. Second, perception of elements that describe the affordances, which can be visual, sonorous or tactile. Putting these three affordances together is central to different degrees of action, inherent to each role the individual performs.

Affordances determine the level of interaction within a given workpiece, analysable in accordance with the *axis of comprehension*. Through HCI axis, the level of engagement and action facing a technology diminishes in each role, inclining to inertia[1] in Audience role – e.g. when the person only watches TV comfortably, almost without taking any action towards the technology. Following this scale, inertia can be total in moments of total distraction, when the viewer does not pay attention to the programme and use the TV set as an environmental sound or company [16]. Therefore, the design of audiovisual workpieces starts from a whole participation (creation/production) to a continuous reduction of actions. As the line advances, strategic functions of HCI resources drop, while relevance of Media Studies increases.

On the other hand, the axis of comprehension through Media Studies involves increasing engagement and action with technology, as the individual develops a more active attitude as roles advance. This is to say that this line starts at inert Audience posture to a higher activity level in every role. The peak of engagement or action is the creative and productive act performed by Modifiers or Producers. The same occurs when one tries to understand narrative complexity and production process domain. While Audience role does not require skills and competencies related to production, the roles with greater activity entail complex actions facing technologies and markets. In this case, the peak of activity is represented by the enhanced role 'Player', which use most of the resources available to each role they are connected to.

Affordances, as approached in the design of audiovisual workpieces, are responsible for calls to action or to inertia, so they form triggers for activity or relaxation. Therefore, we may have Triggers of Action (ToA) and Triggers of Inertia (ToI), which must be considered and included in each phase of design of a production. ToA can be composed by elements of visual signalling, storytelling motivation, narrative curiosity, voice or call for action from a character, desire for more information, game challenges or scavenger hunts, etc. They are subject to a coherent and combined use of the four types of *affordances*, since comprehension issues related to any affordance, even if partial, can compromise the entire experience. On the other hand, ToI normally are present in central points of the story, requiring Audience to present a high level of attentiveness. In this case, perception of ToI may be unconscious, thus not demanding any *functional affordance*. In other cases of increasing inertia (e.g., when the Modifier changes his or her role to Synthesiser), difference of action and of reach of action are conscious to the individual.

Analysing the axis of comprehension through Media Studies, one may note that the first ToA are already present in Audience role, allowing the change into Synthesiser. To understand functioning and reach of action of sharing represents an initial competency of this role. *Functional affordances* are more relevant in this scenario, since they enable decision-making process related to value and outcomes of the interaction. Yet, to move from the roles of Producer, Modifier or Synthesiser to the role of Audience requires ToI, which can be a process more difficult to design.

Finally, it is important to highlight that, to AD, the comprehension of available interaction resources goes through Hartson's four types of affordances [11]. Meanings,

---

[1] In this essay, the word 'inertia' differs from the concept of passivity, broadly discussed in Communication Theories. While the second refers to how people introject content, the former refers to perception and action in response to triggers and related affordances.

especially of *physical affordances*, must be introjected by individuals. The complexity showed in production and enjoyment of contemporary audiovisual works, inherent to the spreadable communication model mentioned above, rises as many persons perform the four AD-assigned roles, simultaneously or in alternated moments. As a result, roles with greater action level help to develop perception by roles of greater inertia.

Besides, *folksonomy* – the moral economy that drives a great deal of actions and can be considered a motivation for acting in roles of greater action level – also discuss the expansion of meanings among people integrating the same network. Circularity of production, providing that Producers appropriate and replicate contributions by fans that are, on their turn, Synthesisers or Modifiers, is an important and efficient key especially from the second level on (Synthesisers). The outcome of such appropriation improves the entire chain of production, with a design adequate to all roles; including Audience, that even if they show the lesser contribution to improvement, benefits from different generations or versions of the product.

4 Learning Affordances

The initial conceptualisation of affordances presumed learning as unnecessary [8]. By looking at an object one should be able to promptly and mechanically know how to use it. According to Kaptelinin [7], this is the main reason why the term rapidly disseminated amongst HCI designers and planners. Such understanding is valid, for instance, for Audience role, given that actions of watching TV or enjoying an audiovisual workpiece, for example, does not rely on complex technological skills or competencies. The presence of *physical affordances* is limited, being representative for AD only when Audience is changing role to Synthesiser, or when Player-Audience makes use of interactive tools.

However, as stated before, contemporary media ecosystem provides natural environment for people to learn, acquire or develop new competencies. Nonetheless, we must bear in mind at least some of the ways that learning occurs. For instance, the Producer may have to enable acquisition of knowledge and skills by users. The design of a complex interactive audiovisual production must foresee affordances that are learnable by the target audience, intuitively and harmonically with the overall universe of the narrative and storytelling. In other words, if the Producer wants (controllable) groups of Synthesisers and Modifiers under a participative and collaborative sense, then the product (content plus interfaces) must present affordances for people to learn how to develop these roles.

Included or not in the Producer's strategy, other learning scenario is relationship among people, who use formal or personal channels to exchange knowledge and experiences about fulfilment of phases and processes inherent to a mediatic product. Consequently, *functional*, *cognitive* and *sensory affordances* may be referred to in terms of interaction contexts, since exchange of information between people improves overall comprehension.

The media environment evolved exploring learning through the support itself. For instance, the first cinema in the beginning of 20th Century had 'lecturers' and 'explicators' during screening, to introduce the then new media affordances to the public –little used to the new format. In today's movies, trailers and teasers tangled with marketing actions afford people to acquire knowledge and capabilities to the moment when the movie is brought into fruition.

About learning and use of software, resources such as visual presentation and tour over validation environment are common, aiming to introduce the set of phases and process of use, using both native resources and advanced devices such as cameras, microphones and sensors. The relationship between audiovisual media and computational software can be illustrated by digital games that supply the person with presentation or introductory sections, test of resources and exploration of technical and conceptual environment simultaneously, allowing the individual to establish aptness levels to expand his or her enjoyment and trigger the alternation of roles.

A complex interactive audiovisual workpiece must present affordances that are adaptable, so the intended audience can intuitively learn them. This characteristic possible both if we consider '*in-use design*' and '*for-use design*', given that the Producer offers an environment with designed affordances. *In-use design* stands for discovery of new uses, or new affordances, by the individual while he or she is enjoying content or using an interface; *for-use design* is the discovery of affordances already predicted by the Producer [17]. The first case is exemplified by resources not foreseeing by designers when conceiving artefacts or, according to the approach we are giving in the present paper, during the conception of an audiovisual workpiece's script. Even so, exploration of the environment is an individuals' duty, who may fully or partially comply with it, or even aggregate new meanings. In extreme situations, the person can notice affordances that were not planned by the Producer, making enjoyment of the audiovisual product even more complex. Concerning the Player – the enhanced role responsible for taking the most extreme actions when consuming audiovisual product – the constant quest for novelties encourages creation of new affordances, thus increasing storytelling power. Subsequently, learning affordances (especially *cognitive* ones) is important for a good experience in each role performed by the individual.

The learning process can also be developed through conceptual approaches – e.g. Media Literacy – which propose teaching of social, economic, technical and cultural aspects of media usage, to expand competencies of access, analysis and creation of content. To conclude, the complex nature of relationships between affordances and individuals can be addressed through contributions to interaction design by the Theory of Activity[2], which considers each element via encounter of distinct levels: Artefact > Tool > User interface *Versus* User < Worked < Human Being [18]. That is, the Producer constructs an artefact with a set of affordances to individuals, who construct their connection to the media in accordance to human factors (motivations, experiences), and conduct action to attain objectives and activities. This way, *in-use design* can differ from the scenario predicted by *for-use design*.

---

[2] Affordances are not really addressed in the Theory of Activity, but this approximation is important for the AD, to understand the complexity of possible actions within each role.

5 Conclusion

This essay has introduced the concept of affordances in Audiovisual Design methodology. The term is central and necessary for comprehension of actions individuals can take when they occupy each role assigned by the AD. It is also important for planning audiovisual workpieces, both in terms of production – when affordances become a tool of action or inertia – and in terms of engagement innate to Synthesiser and Modifier roles. Affordances can be understood as characteristics of an object that can be perceived in its integrity, or that must be complemented by the individual's perception. This analysis is not central to AD, since the model focuses on triggers for alternating roles: a reduction to a level of greater inertia, or a progression to roles of greater activity and engagement.

Contemporary media ecosystem, by converging different media in the same environment, dominated by digital technology, brings new demands for interaction, resulting in the rise of new affordances, related to use of interfaces and computers. Therefore, HCI Studies contributes with analysis of situations in which media consumption takes place, providing methodologies to underline and explain which the new affordances are and how audiovisual production must be organised around them. Therefore, it becomes possible to predict, during the design of programmes, content and interaction interfaces, actions to be taken by individuals. The problem-solution chain of HCI allows the advent of a complex use of different media and platforms, by indicating potential features of each content-distribution channel.

This initial discussion about affordances brought several questions to be approached in future works. First, a detailed investigation and listing of most relevant affordances, accompanied by incorporation of further discussions on theories, especially about concepts of *hidden* and *functional* affordances. It must also be specified how Producers must address to unpredicted uses and appropriation of technology and content, which is already suggested by the Theory of Activity, and the contrast between *design for use* and *design in use* – concepts that must be better incorporated by AD. Such study will help to further develop behaviours and competencies related to Players. Also, future investigations must apply these theories into concrete productions and analysis of actual content, especially to show how competencies are acquired by individuals, and how media affordances can be transformed into real, viable tools. Another line of investigation is delimiting the technologies and affordances required for a full implementation of interactive TV.

Although the AD methodology considers currently available technologies, we must keep an open plan to incorporate new social and technological dynamics that can modify the proposed workflow. We also understand that economic restrictions can render inviable the complete application of this methodology in its full version in every audiovisual production. Nonetheless, Audiovisual Design remains a valid methodological set since it allows to contemplate every phase of the design process as an isolated process. Also, it adds elements to the debate about formation of professionals who will produce this type of content, demonstrating the need for a revision of scholar curricula, especially in careers of audiovisual production, which currently does not contemplate subjects important to the producer of content for interactive systems.

Acknowledgement. Daniel Gambaro recognises and thanks São Paulo Estate Research Foundation - FAPESP, for grants received, to which this and other researches are connected: Processes 2015/20430-5 and 2016/17884-7.

References

1. Becker, V., Gambaro, D., Ramos, T.S.: Audiovisual design and the convergence between HCI and audience studies. In: Kurosu, M. (ed.) HCI 2017. LNCS, vol. 10271, pp. 3–22. Springer, Cham (2017). https://doi.org/10.1007/978-3-319-58071-5_1
2. Norman, D.A.: The Psychology of Everyday Things. Basic Books, New York (1988)
3. Souza, J.P.: Elementos de Teoria e Pesquisa da Comunicação e dos Media, 2nd edn. Edições Universidade Fernando Pessoa, Porto (PT) (2006)
4. Jenkins, H., Ford, S., Green, J.: Spreadable Media: Creating Value and Meaning in a Networked Culture (Kindle Edition). New York University Press, New York (2013)
5. Gaver, W.W.: Technology affordances. In: Proceedings of the SIGCHI Conference on Human Factors in Computing Systems (CHI 1991), pp. 79–84 (1991). https://doi.org/10.1145/108844.108856
6. Strate, L.: A media ecology review. In: Communication Research Trends - Centre for the Study of Communication and Culture, vol. 23, no. 2, pp. 3–48 (2004). https://goo.gl/t7CmP6
7. Kaptelinin, V.: Affordances and Design. The Interaction Design Foundation (2014)
8. Gibson, J.J.: The theory of affordances. In: Shaw, R., Bransford, J. (eds.) Perceiving, Acting and Knowing. Lawrence Erlbaum, Hillsdale (1977)
9. Gibson, J.J.: The Ecological Approach to Visual Perception. Lawrence Erlbaum Associates, New Jersey (1979)
10. Gibson, E.J., Pick, A.D.: An Ecological Approach to Perceptual Learning and Development. Oxford University Press, Cary (2003)
11. Hartson, H.R.: Cognitive, physical, sensory, and functional affordances in interaction design. Behav. Inf. Technol. **22**(5), 315–338 (2003). https://doi.org/10.1080/01449290310001592587
12. Woodruffe, C.: What is meant by a competency? Leadersh. Organ. Dev. J. **14**(1), 29–36 (1993). https://doi.org/10.1108/eb053651
13. Boyatzis, R.E.: Competencies in the 21st century. J. Manag. Dev. **27**(1), 5–12 (2008). https://doi.org/10.1108/02621710810840730
14. Yoon, C.Y.: The effect factors of end-user task performance in a business environment: focusing on computing competency. Comput. Hum. Behav. **25**(6), 1207–1212 (2009). https://doi.org/10.1016/j.chb.2009.06.008
15. Becker, V., Fornari, A., Herweg Filho, G.H., Montez, C.: Recomendações de usabilidade para TV digital interativa. In: II WTVD, Proceedings, pp. 27–38 (2006). https://goo.gl/bBgbWT
16. Machado, A.: A televisão levada a sério. Senac, São Paulo (2003)
17. Folcher, V.: Appropriating artefacts as instruments: when design-for-use meets design-in-use. Interact. Comput. **15**(5), 647–663 (2003). https://doi.org/10.1016/S0953-5438(03)00057-2
18. Kaptelinin, V., Nardi, B.A.: Acting with Technology: Activity Theory and Interaction Design. MIT Press, Cambridge (2006)

Application for Older Adults to Ask for Help from Volunteers Through Television: Design and Evaluation of a High Visual-Fidelity Prototype

Tânia Ribeiro[1] , Rita Santos[2,3]([✉]) , João Moura[1] , Ana Isabel Martins[4,5] , and Hilma Caravau[3,4]

[1] Communication and Art Department, University of Aveiro, Aveiro, Portugal
ribeirotania@ua.pt, moura.jps@gmail.com
[2] Águeda School of Technology and Management, University of Aveiro, Aveiro, Portugal
rita.santos@ua.pt
[3] CIC.DIGITAL/Digimedia, University of Aveiro, Aveiro, Portugal
hilmacaravau90@gmail.com
[4] National Association of Gerontologists, University of Aveiro, Aveiro, Portugal
anaisabelmartins@gmail.com
[5] Institute of Electronics and Telematics Engineering of Aveiro, Aveiro, Portugal

Abstract. Designing a television (TV) application for older adults presents specific challenges, especially when the issue is an application that aims to support volunteer activities which will benefit older adults. This article describes the design process and evaluation of an interactive high visual-fidelity prototype of an application for a TV set-top box, which aims to allow older adults to request, in a simple and quick way, help from a group of volunteers, in specific tasks such as small household maintenance. Concerning the user interface design, a set of specific guidelines were considered and applied in the development of a high visual-fidelity prototype. The result of this process was later evaluated in heuristic evaluation sessions and user testing. The former were supported by a list of heuristics, drawn from other lists used in recent research and adapted to the context of the study. The latter were conducted with potential users that tried to accomplish some tasks on the prototype. In a context in which several studies show that television is a highly privileged platform to provide information to the older adults population due to its high degree of use in this group, this project may present important contributions to better understand some of the challenges that are associated with the design and early evaluation of TV applications whose target audience is older adults and some good practices that should be followed to achieve a product that is easy and enjoyable for this public to use.

Keywords: Iterative design · User interface design · Heuristic evaluation
User testing · Application for set-top TV box · Volunteering

© Springer International Publishing AG, part of Springer Nature 2018
M. J. Abásolo et al. (Eds.): jAUTI 2017, CCIS 813, pp. 32–43, 2018.
https://doi.org/10.1007/978-3-319-90170-1_3

1 Introduction

The aging process is often associated with dependency, financial difficulties, loneliness and isolation [1]. In Portugal, about 60% of the older adults population live alone or in the exclusive company of other older adults, which reflects a phenomenon of social isolation whose dimension has increased around 28% over the last decade [2]. Even if older adults stay at home (which is commonly a sign of a good health situation), there are innumerable difficulties that they cannot overcome alone. Many times, these situations can be avoided if older adults are supported by other people that help them, for example, performing daily living activities.

Voluntary actions accomplishment is one way to fulfil situations of exclusion and social isolation and, at the same time, promotes independence, autonomy, quality of life and socialization of older adults. It is possible to notice that there are already several Information and Communication Technology applications that aim to support voluntary actions, especially Web/mobile. However, many of these applications do not seem to give a special importance to the characteristics, preferences and needs of older adults. In particular, it can be seen that the use of television (TV) as a platform to support requests to volunteers seems to be a poorly studied scenario, although TV is one of the means with the greatest penetration in Portuguese homes and with which individuals, over 64 years old, are highly familiar with [3, 4].

It is against this background, and considering the results of a questionnaire to better know how key stakeholders see the relevance and some requirements of a TV application to support volunteering targeting older adults (topic not elaborated in this article), that arises the VoluntAge4Seniors project, a research project whose purpose is to develop an application to run in a specific TV set-top box that aims, in a simple and quick way, to allow older adults to request help from a group of volunteers in daily living tasks (such as a ride to the supermarket or do simple household arrangements such as change a lamp). This request will be made by entering the request and its details (such as category, date, time and location) by a TV remote control or through voice. The main objective of the voice interaction is to simplify the process of asking for help, considering the difficulties that often arise through the use of TV remote control [5]. It is important to note that voice interfaces are not yet common, despite their recognized potential to ease daily living for older adults [6]. The TV application will also allow older adults to evaluate the help they have been given.

To ensure that technological solutions fulfil the needs and expectations of their target audience and, at the same time, guarantee that the products are easy to use, it is recommended to follow an iterative cycle of design-evaluate-redesign from initial ideas through various prototypes to the final product [7]. Indeed, assuring high levels of usability is a critical aspect because it has a direct interference with decisions around adoption and use of technology-enabled products and services [8]. To achieve this, applying Human Computer Interaction (HCI) principles and guidelines when creating prototypes and identify usability problems in these artefacts in the context of usability evaluations is of the most importance.

It is under this scope that the authors developed a high visual fidelity prototype considering a set of User Interface (UI) design principles. In addition to this, an evaluation of the prototype's usability was carried out using heuristic evaluation and user testing. The results of these activities are here presented, aiming to contribute to a more informed design of TV interfaces, in similar contexts to the one that was approached under the scope of the VoluntAge4Seniors project.

2   Considerations About the Design of TV Interfaces for Older Adults and Its Evaluation

When designing an application for older adults, it is important to take into consideration that older adults do not belong to a well-defined category of users and that they are not considerably different from other categories of users, as presented in most HCI work [9]. Furthermore, it should be taken into account that some UI design guidelines for a standard laptop cannot be applied to the television [10].

As a result, for the design of the prototype, a comprehensive set of guidelines were considered, from a set of general guidelines for UI design [11, 12] to others that approach the design of interfaces for Interactive TV [13] or for older adults [14], or even specifically address the design of interfaces for TV UI for older adults [15].

From this revision of guidelines, several important aspects had emerged, many of them related with the biologic changes that typically appear in the aging process [14]. One that should be highlighted is the attention that should be paid to ensure that the number of steps it takes to reach a given screen is the minimum possible and the design of the application must be consistent to facilitate recognition, avoiding the overload of the short-term memory. Regarding the information displayed, it must be precise and make use of simple language, in order to give users time to read and focus on a single task at a time [14]. In terms of visibility, the interface must clearly show in which stage of the application the user is and which is the current selection or the possible interaction available [13]. Apart from the usage of simple and precise information, meaningful icons and labels also help in this task [11, 12]. To achieve readability, the typography must be large, sans serif and the text must be left aligned [4, 7].

Besides these guidelines being widely recognized as effective, it is essential to evaluate the interface design where they are applied even because this could help to refine the guidelines to better adapt to specific contexts. Heuristic evaluation has been recognized as a popular usability inspection technique, where one of its main advantages is that it can be used at any stage of a design project, including in an early stage of design [7]. With respect to usability heuristics that can be used in the evaluation of UI targeted at older adults, it is observed that new lists of heuristics had even emerged from Nielsen's list of heuristics [11] to better recognize any potential issues. Besides the importance of carrying out heuristic evaluation, there is a widely recognized importance of involving the potential users of an application in early-and late-stage usability testing. This is particularly important in the case of users with age-related changes in hearing, vision, cognition, and mobility.

3 The High Visual-Fidelity Prototype

Besides the guidelines mentioned in the previous section, a set of practices pointed by the staff of the TV service company responsible for the development of the general environment provided by the set-top box were also considered. One example of this is the need to create a "safe area" (around 20% of the total space) all around the screen without any content. Considering this information, a nonfunctional high visual-fidelity prototype, with some content simulating the real one, was developed using a popular vector illustration tool (Adobe Illustrator).

At the end of a first version of the prototype, the result was discussed with two people of the TV service company with great responsibility in the team that develops the environment and apps of the set-top box. Important feedback about some design options was received. One example was that some screens had a lot of information, even when particular care was taken with this issue since the beginning.

The final version of the high visual-fidelity prototype included the most important features: Selection of profile and Login; Home, area where the user could see potential pendent actions (such as evaluate a volunteer and/or confirm the help offered from a volunteer); Requests, area where the user could make a new request, see the requests scheduled (already accepted or not from a volunteer); New request: area where the user could start to choose the category of the request and, in subsequent steps, could choose the type of input (voice or TV remote control) and see information to help him to make the request by voice and: Profile, where user could see their personal data and statistics related with the use of the application.

Figure 1 shows the *Request* area, where the user decides to do a new volunteer request. After this, the user selects the category of the request as illustrated in Fig. 2.

Fig. 1. Request area: choice of new request.

The interface design, followed in almost all other interfaces, aimed to be minimalist, with short and meaningful information. Every menu option had its name, and a correspondent icon, to facilitate the memorization. It is also possible to see that the interface showed clearly the current location (in the left menu lighted in green) and that it had considerable negative space, to facilitate the choice of a category and the finding of the information by the user. In the main area, the selected content was highlighted with color whereas the other elements were represented in gray.

Fig. 2. New request: category selection. (Color figure online)

The system triggered confirmation/alert messages in the final decision-making situations. These messages occupied the whole screen of the TV, which means the side menu did not appear, avoiding misinterpretations by the user. In addition, the user had to do some action on every message that appeared on the screen making sure he had time to read all the information presented. Figure 3 shows an example of the resume screen that appeared after making a request. The user had to validate or edit the request to continue using the application.

Fig. 3. Request feedback.

4 Evaluation Sessions

In the evaluation sessions, to make the prototype presented in the previous section to look and feel more like the end-product, some interactivity was added using Invision, a rapid prototyping cloud application that allows to transform a static design into a clickable and interactive prototype.

The prototype was evaluated in three heuristic evaluation sessions (described in Sect. 4.1) and two user tests (described in Sect. 4.2). The aim of these sessions was evaluating the UI design and recognizing any potential issues and usability problems.

Table 1. List of heuristics

Content	
H1	Provides clear feedback and when presenting error messages make them simple and easy to follow
H2	The errors messages are descriptive and use meaningful words and verbs when requiring an action
H3	Used language is simple, clear and adequate to users
Navigation	
H4	The user interface navigation structure is clear, simple and straightforward
H5	The "cancel" button behaves in a predictable manner
H6	Promotes user control and freedom, allowing for alternative and flexible flows of interaction
H7	Disable options are inactive
Dexterity	
H8	Avoids pull down menus
H9	Avoids the use of scrolling
H10	Large sized user interface elements in general
Cognition	
H11	Focus on one task at a time instead of requiring the user to actively monitor two or more tasks, and clearly indicates the name and status of the task at all times
H12	Avoid the use of interaction timeouts and provide ample time to read information
H13	Provide familiar mental models
H14	Supports recognition rather than recall
H15	Uses pictures and/or graphics purposefully and adequately to minimize user interface clutter and avoid extraneous details
Perception	
H16	Does not rely on color alone to convey information. Be aware of color blindness
H17	Makes information accessible through different modalities
H18	Provides a good contrast between background and content
H19	The background is consistent among all sections
H20	Reduces the demand on working memory by supporting recognition rather than recall
H21	Unambiguously shows the user's location
Aesthetic	
H22	Ensures that text types, styles and sizes are appropriate to users, that is, for instance, but not exclusively: large-sized fonts, sans serif, non-condensed typefaces, non-italic
H23	Buttons are clearly visible and distinguishable from other user interface elements
H24	Information is visually grouped (makes good use of color, text, topics, etc.)
H25	Provides sufficient space between elements to ensure a balanced user interface design
H26	Uses simple and meaningful icons

4.1 Heuristic Evaluation Sessions

A list of heuristics was developed based on a set of heuristics suggested by [10, 17] where Nielsen's heuristics have an important role. At the end of a first version of the list, an expert in TV applications development was asked to give feedback about the list and some changes were made.

Table 1 presents the final heuristics list that was used in the heuristic evaluation sessions.

For the evaluation, a laptop was used to present the prototype and record the audio from the sessions as well as the screen activity. The evaluation sessions were conducted with people with background in HCI (number of three). All had at least some experience in developing heuristic evaluations and interfaces for older adults. One of the participants did not have experience with development of TV applications. The heuristic evaluation session developed in three distinct main stages: (1) set the context to the evaluator regarding the application usage scenarios, interface functionalities that were considered in the prototype and adopted heuristics; (2) the heuristic evaluation itself over the prototype. As recommended by Nielsen [17], the evaluator firstly explored the interface freely and secondly focused on specific interface elements and report. As they went through the interface, evaluators verbalized the problems identified, the usability principles that were violated and suggestions of solutions while an observer registered them in a grid; (3) the evaluator answered a questionnaire about his/her profile and, in open questions, pointed the interface strengths and limitations.

4.2   User Testing

Besides considering important to carry out a heuristic evaluation, the prototype assessment near potential end-users was also considered central to complement the heuristic evaluation inputs. Therefore, two user tests were conducted with the aim of collecting information concerning key aspects that should be improved, both in terms of visual design and features presented in the prototype.

As in the heuristic evaluation, a laptop was used to present the prototype. It was initially foreseen the use of a method resembling Wizard-of-Oz since when the user interacted with TV remote control the user's screen was controlled by one of the members of the team. Besides the responsible researcher making correspondence of the interface's screens with the movements and choices of the user, there was a member that assumed the role of coordinator (responsible for the interaction with the participant) and another researcher that played the observer role (responsible for registering the options taken by the user, comments and suggestions pronounced during on-going tasks and assuring the assembly of the test scenario).

The participants included in this study were selected by convenience among seniors related to the research team. The inclusion criteria considered were: being 60 years old or almost; watching television regularly; knowing how to read.

The tests took place under controlled conditions (laboratory). In the initial part of the test, the objectives of the test, the context of the application and the further use of data collected were explained in detail to each participant. The user also had the opportunity to request additional information and was aware that he could quit anytime. Additionally, an information sheet was given, and each participant was asked to sign an informed consent. Afterwards, the participant was invited to perform a list of eight tasks: (1) enter the application with a specific profile; (2) make a new request for help; (3)

change the date of previous request; (4) evaluate one specific volunteer; (5) accept help from one volunteer; (6) check profile information; (7) check his previous requests for help and; (8) exit the application. Following a thinking aloud method, it was requested that the user verbalize his thoughts as he moved through the user interface. Simultaneously, the observer registered the participants' actions and the observations considered relevant that occurred during each task. At the end of the test, a questionnaire was applied including questions about participants' TV consumption habits, level of satisfaction with the high-fidelity prototype tested, utility of the application and expected usefulness of the voice interaction.

5   Results and Discussion

The results from the evaluation session are presented according to the typology of evaluation carried out.

5.1   Heuristic Evaluation

The data collected in the sessions was compiled and analyzed to identify the major usability problems and problematic aspects of the design. Table 2 presents major findings of these analysis, following a similar approach as the one presented in Silva *et al.* [10].

Table 2. Violated heuristics (amount of violations)

Most violated heuristics overall							
H3 (19)							
H13 (12)							
H1 (9)							
H4 (9)							

Violated heuristics of the main screens								
	Login	Home	Volunteer evaluation	Volunteer confirmation	Requests	Make a request by voice	Edit request	Profile
	H1 (2)	H3 (5)	H13 (2)	H3 (5)	H1 (2)	H4 (2)	H3 (2)	H3 (3)
	H3 (2)	H13 (3)	H4 (1)	H13 (3)	H3 (2)			H1 (1)
	H13 (2)	H1 (2)	H11 (1)	H1 (2)	H13 (2)			H21 (1)
	H4 (1)	H4 (2)	H20 (1)	H4 (2)	H26 (2)			
	H18 (1)	H20 (2)		H21 (1)	H4 (1)			
		H11 (1)		H24 (1)				
		H24 (1)						
Total	8	**16**	5	**14**	9	2	2	5

It can be observed that the most infringed heuristics were H3 (related to clarity of the used language), H13 (related to the familiarity of the application mental model), H1 (related to feedback clearness) and H4 (related to navigation clearness). This data can be accessed in Table 2.

The most frequently mentioned problems were related with the overuse of text using bullets, the selection area that moved in the screen instead of the content and the fact that in some areas the text missed clarity and simplicity.

The absence of records in some heuristics (e.g. H2, H5 and H7) may have different interpretations. This can be related with the lack of elements in the interface where these heuristics could be applied or even with the preference for other heuristics by the evaluators to describe a certain usability issue.

The questionnaire filled by the three evaluators pointed out strengths such as the project goals, the possibility of interaction using voice, the consistency of the interfaces, the fact that the interfaces focused on a single action at a time, adequate font types and sizes and general navigation. The most critical weaknesses highlighted were about how older adults were asked to interact by voice and excessive density of information for a TV UI in some screens.

5.2   User Testing

Three participants were recruited to participate in the user tests, but one did not agree to provide some personal information to be used in the context of the study nor sign the informed consent. This person tried to accomplish the proposed set of tasks but after having some difficulties in the first two tasks decided not to continue the test. The two other participants took their involvement in the study very seriously and carried out the tests to the end. The first participant was 59, male, and the second was 82, female. Both had paid TV and the second participant referred to using the TV set-top box to schedule recordings, to see television programming and see past programs.

During the tests, the use of the technique resembling Wizard-of-Oz revealed not to be very functional and intuitive, with the mouse cursor being a distraction to the users. The problem was worsened by the fact that some network problems happened causing the restart of the application. Despite this, some major results emerged regarding the interface design and usability. These include: the relevance of replace the term "Help", used in the application to provide more information about the application, since it was suggesting an option to start an ask for help; the choice of the green color in the context of a selected element seemed to work fine in the overall although more differentiation with other contents would be desired by using, for example, blinking; language expressions that were not completely intuitive to the users; the side menu became distractive in some tasks according to participant 2; the use of circles as a visual clue for showing the step in the task (Fig. 2) did not prove to be useful; participant 2 pointed out the lack of a return button in a certain screen and; the participant 2 mentioned two functionalities that, according to her, were not in proper locations.

In the final questionnaire, both participants that accomplished the given tasks said, using a 5-point Likert scale, to like the application experience and they agreed in classifying it as useful. One of the participants promptly classified the speech-to-text feature as useful while the other one showed to be reluctant concerning using this technology, admitting however that speech-to-text process is easier than using the TV remote control keys. The former participant also admitted considering the use of the application in the future while the other one user-tester pointed that he would hardly use the application.

6 Conclusions and Future Work

This article presented the results of the design and evaluation of a high-visual fidelity prototype of a TV application that will support older adults to request help from a group of volunteers in daily living tasks. Both design guidelines and the two types of evaluation proved to be fruitful to design and assess problems, specially related with the visual part, of TV applications that will be used by older adults.

Regarding design, a set of guidelines from distinct categories and from diverse backgrounds was taken into consideration. Although there are already some studies that present design recommendations for TV for older adults in similar contexts of the project here presented, it is considered that the results of this work are an important contribution to the validation of these recommendations. The validation of the design with professionals from the TV company, with a vast experience in TV applications development, also proved to be beneficial, allowing the identification of some issues that could be revealed in problems in the context of use.

The heuristic evaluation was also an important contribute not only because of the input that was given before initiating the implementation of the application but also because the heuristics list that supported the evaluation. A list of 26 heuristics was developed based on other lists and adapted to support the main potential usability problems that could arise in the UI developed. The results reinforced the importance, pointed by Nielsen [9], of considering not only a standard list of heuristics to support the development and evaluation of more specific products as the one here presented. Despite the low number of potential users, user testing with the two older adults in an early stage of design revealed to be an interesting method to complement heuristic evaluation and an essential step to develop a product that meets users' needs and expectations and with a high degree of acceptance. Nevertheless, it would have been useful to use co-design with older adults in the definition of the application UI, for example in the identification of language expressions to be used in the application since several issues showed that the language used was not completely intuitive to the users.

In general, the procedures followed in the evaluation sessions were revealed as adequate but further analysis should be done towards the validation of the heuristic evaluation method that was used in different scenarios. In terms of less positive aspects, the Wizard-of-Oz approach that was used as well as the use of a cloud solution to present the prototype proved not to be very adequate for doing tests with older adults causing interruptions in the interaction with the application.

As improvements, the authors recommend reducing the number of heuristics to become easier for evaluators to remember. Also, it would have been useful to perform the evaluation using a TV screen and remote control.

Regarding future work, it is aimed to continue the TV application development, considering the findings from the tests described in this article to improve the UI component. Another major step will be to better understand how the ask for help using voice should be undertaken in the context of a TV application. It is aimed to undertake these actions by continuing to use an iterative design approach given its proven benefits to development lifecycle.

Acknowledgments. The research leading to this work received funding from AlticeLabs@UA. The authors would like to thank the support provided by the National Association of Gerontologists (Associação Nacional de Gerontólogos - ANG) for their contribution to this paper and for the collaboration in this research in general.

References

1. Silva, T., Abreu, J., Antunes, M., Almeida, P., Silva, V., Santinha, G.: +TV4E: interactive television as a support to push information about social services to the elderly. In: Conference on Health and Social Care Information Systems and Technologies, CENTERIS, pp. 1–6 (2016)
2. Instituto Nacional de Estatística: Censos 2011: Resultados Definitivos - Portugal, Lisboa, Portugal (2012)
3. Entidade Reguladora para a Comunicação Social: As novas dinâmicas do consumo audiovisual em Portugal 2016, Lisboa (2016)
4. Marktest Group: Portugueses viram cerca de 3h30m de Tv em 2010. http://www.marktest.com/wap/a/n/id~16e0.aspx
5. Ribeiro, V.S., Martins, A.I., Queirós, A., Silva, A.G., Rocha, N.P.: Usability evaluation of a health care application based on IPTV. Procedia Comput. Sci. **64**, 635–642 (2015). https://doi.org/10.1016/j.procs.2015.08.577
6. Portet, F., Vacher, M., Golanski, C., Roux, C., Meillon, B.: Design and evaluation of a smart home voice interface for the elderly: acceptability and objection aspects. Pers. Ubiquit. Comput. **17**, 127–144 (2013). https://doi.org/10.1007/s00779-011-0470-5
7. Preece, J., Rogers, Y., Sharp, H.: Beyond Interaction Design: Beyond Human-Computer Interaction. Wiley, New York (2015)
8. Lee, C., Coughlin, J.F.: Perspective: older adults' adoption of technology: an integrated approach to identifying determinants and barriers. J. Prod. Innov. Manag. **32**, 747–759 (2014)
9. Righi, V., Sayago, S., Blat, J.: When we talk about older people in HCI, who are we talking about? Towards a "turn to community" in the design of technologies for a growing ageing population. Int. J. Hum Comput Stud. **108**, 15–31 (2017). https://doi.org/10.1016/j.ijhcs.2017.06.005
10. Silva, P.A., Holden, K., Jordan, P.: Towards a list of heuristics to evaluate smartphone apps targeted at older adults: a study with apps that aim at promoting health and well-being. In: Proceedings Annual Hawaii International Conference System Science, March 2015, pp. 3237–3246 (2015). https://doi.org/10.1109/hicss.2015.390
11. Molich, R., Nielsen, J.: Improving a human-computer dialogue. Commun. ACM **33**, 338–348 (1990). https://doi.org/10.1145/77481.77486
12. Nielsen, J., Molich, R.: Heuristic evaluation of user interfaces. In: Proceedings of the SIGCHI Conference on Human Factors in Computing Systems Empowering People - CHI 1990, pp. 249–256. ACM Press, New York (1990)
13. Chorianopoulos, K.: User interface design principles for interactive television applications. Int. J. Hum. Comput. Interact. **24**, 556–573 (2008). https://doi.org/10.1080/10447310802205750

14. Pak, R., McLaughlin, A.: Designing Displays for Older Adults. CRC Press, Boca Raton (2010)
15. Nunes, F., Kerwin, M., Silva, P.A.: Design recommendations for TV user interfaces for older adults: findings from the eCAALYX project. In: Proceedings 14th International ACM SIGACCESS Conference Computer Access. - ASSETS 2012, p. 41 (2012). https://doi.org/10.1145/2384916.2384924
16. Van Barneveld, J., Van Setten, M.: Designing usable interfaces for TV recommender systems. Hum.-Comput. Interact. **6**, 259–286 (2004). https://doi.org/10.1007/1-4020-2164-X_10
17. Nielsen, J.: How to conduct a heuristic evaluation. https://www.nngroup.com/articles/how-to-conduct-a-heuristic-evaluation/

Iterative User Experience Evaluation of a User Interface for the Unification of TV Contents

Pedro Almeida$^{(\boxtimes)}$ ⓘ, Jorge Abreu$^{(\boxtimes)}$ ⓘ, Telmo Silva$^{(\boxtimes)}$ ⓘ,
Enrickson Varsori ⓘ, Eliza Oliveira ⓘ, Ana Velhinho ⓘ,
Sílvia Fernandes ⓘ, Rafael Guedes ⓘ, and Diogo Oliveira ⓘ

CIC.DIGITAL/Digimedia, Department of Communication and Arts,
University of Aveiro, Aveiro, Portugal
{almeida,jfa,tsilva,varsori,elizaoliveira,
ana.velhinho,silvia.fernandes,rafaelguedes,
diogo.guerreiro}@ua.pt

Abstract. One of the key components of the design and development process of a User Interface (UI) is the User Experience (UX) assessment. It guarantees that the product meets the users' needs and provides the best interaction, while achieving usability goals and emotional reactions of motivation, arousal and dominance. In this scope, this paper describes the results driven from a User-Centered Design (UCD) methodology adopted in the development and evaluation of consecutive versions of semi-functional prototypes (of the UltraTV concept), with iterations that comprised an expert review and subsequent testing with users in a laboratory environment. This evaluation approach aims to achieve a proof of concept for the profile-based unification of traditional TV and Over-the-top contents offered in the same user interface. As an R&D project based on a partnership between the research field and the industry that aims to bring innovation to the interactive TV (iTV) domain, the UltraTV concept targets for the synergy between users and market interests. Despite the challenges of introducing an interface that unifies linear and nonlinear content in the same UI assuring the continuity of the UX contrary to the current app-based trend, the combined results from the experts' review and the inLab tests demonstrate the relevance and desirability of the concept as a potential solution for the future of iTV. The presented results provide valuable insights for further stages of field trials with end users, as well as to prove the feasibility and user demand for the profile-based unification for the next TV generation.

Keywords: Interactive television · Prototype evaluation · User interface
User experience · Content unification

1 Introduction

The development of a system corresponds to an iteration process, as it considers opinions from different evaluators, in distinct phases of the prototypes, for identifying issues to be improved and enhancing the global user experience [1].

Additionally, it is crucial to the success of a system to timely test it, since its development benefits substantially from the gathered insights. These tests also offer the

© Springer International Publishing AG, part of Springer Nature 2018
M. J. Abásolo et al. (Eds.): jAUTI 2017, CCIS 813, pp. 44–57, 2018.
https://doi.org/10.1007/978-3-319-90170-1_4

opportunity to evaluate design alternatives in low fidelity prototypes, allowing the iterative refinement of different versions presented to the evaluators [2].

A review by experts plays an important role in this process, as it provides access to the evaluators' professional experience (simultaneously as developers, researchers and users), representing a value-added assessment at both levels: in the development process and in a final solution. Additionally, laboratory tests can simulate a domestic environment, providing an experience resembling a real living room, contributing for gathering suggestions to make improvements in the system and guarantee the production of a high-fidelity prototype that meets the users' needs. Therefore, a variety of tests should be made throughout the development process [2].

The referred iterative development process has a special relevance in the ongoing academic and industry initiatives that aim to streamline the future of the TV ecosystem. The current television scenario is going through fundamental changes in the way viewers get access to TV contents, increasingly supported by Video On Demand (VoD) services in addition to the traditional lineup of TV contents. This transformation on the viewing habits is supported by recent solutions, granting access to the available contents anytime and anywhere [3, 4]. These solutions include the use of mobile devices, working as secondary screens [3, 5], and many times as the primary displays for watching TV. Also, the services of traditional Pay-TV operators have been trying to adjust to the contemporary scenario. To grant its clients with access to linear contents at alternative schedules, Pay-TV operators allow pre-programed TV to become more flexible by introducing services like "catch-up TV" and "time-shift" [6, 7]. This framework leads to enormous changes in the TV offer, increasing the challenges of commercial players that are trying to cope with new users' expectations by offering more engaging systems supported on new paradigms of User Interfaces (UI). In this scope, the consortium of the UltraTV project (involving Altice Labs as an IPTV player, University of Aveiro and Instituto de Telecomunicações - a R&D institution in the field of telecommunications) is designing an iTV concept, with the most advanced features on the market, capable of serving as a basis for a new generation of a Pay-TV service.

In this paper, a systematization of the evaluation tests performed to consecutive versions of the UltraTV prototype is presented, addressing two types of tests: a review by five experts, organized in two panels (one in Chicago and the other in Aveiro); and an evaluation in a laboratory environment with 20 participants (which took place during a week in Aveiro). It should be noted that the version of the prototype tested in the lab with users integrated some improvements, resulting from the suggestions of the experts, while other aspects were maintained to test the opinion of the users in order to confirm some of the prior insights. In this sense, two versions of the prototype, designated by Version 1 (tested with experts) and Version 2 (tested inLab with users) are described in this article.

The paper is structured as follows. The next Sect. (2) presents the state of the art concerning current viewing habits, iTV industry trends and User Experience (UX) assessments in the iTV context. In the next section, the UltraTV project is presented based on what was named the "TV Flow", as a foundational concept for a profile-based unification approach translated into a user interface to access content from different sources. Section 3 presents the evaluation goals and methodology used for the validation of the prototypes. In Sect. 4 the results are discussed, namely the assessment made by the experts and the outputs from the inLab tests. Finally, the last Sect. (5) highlights the most relevant considerations and suggestions for future work.

2 State of the Art

2.1 Viewing Habits and Industry Trends

The television scenario has been suffering significant changes, regarding the transformation on viewers' habits. To cope with this new context, Pay-TV operators provide new features to increase enjoyment and to personalize the users' TV experience, such as catch-up TV, time shifted, and Video-on-Demand (VoD). This context is sustained by the growing availability of audiovisual technology [7], which makes it possible to watch any content, anywhere, at any time [4]. From the several UI design approaches leveraged by the iTV industry that try to adjust to the current scenario and provide an engaging experience there are two that are worth being mentioned. Supported by a flexible grid, the Argentine operator Cablevisión[1] proposes a different layout approach with the introduction of the Flow solution, in an all intuitive UI, combining linear content, OTT, Time-shift TV services with content filtering according to a user's preferences. In turn, Android TV[2] proposes the unification of contents from Google sources and for recommendations on the home screen, using a carrousel menu with different contents in a same line and allowing the connection to other Google features.

Moreover, innovative layouts that emphasize the dynamics of the navigation supported by transition effects have been presented, such as the three-dimensional effect in Mur Vidéo[3] by Voo, the diagonal carrousel navigation of the smart TV LG webOS[4], the horizontal navigation with circular items, of Frog[5] interface by Wyplay, or the disruptive interfaces by Cisco, like the Infinite Video Platform[6], based on video masks. All this scenario leads to the hybridization of the ways TV is viewed and provide changes on the paradigm of graphical approaches (centered on layout, typographic treatment, animations, transitions and effects) associated with navigation and visual feedback given to the user, leading to an easy and intuitive but also captivating and immersive UX [8].

2.2 Evaluations in ITV Context

It is possible to relate UX to several different contexts, leading to a nonconsensual concept in what concerns the meaning of the term [9, 10]. Therefore, many are the definitions related to UX, which are strictly related to the issues correlated to the respective individual area. Following this perspective, Law defines UX as follows:

---

[1] Cablevisión Flow: https://www.youtube.com/watch?v=IE0n-WlGHYg.

[2] Android TV: https://www.android.com/tv/.

[3] Voo Mur Vidéo - https://www.youtube.com/watch?v=dwLK2stDH0g.

[4] LG webOS 3.5 - https://www.youtube.com/watch?v=v5471kC8heE.

[5] Wyplay Frog - https://www.youtube.com/watch?v=cNSkoeDaGDY.

[6] Cisco Infinite Video Platform - https://www.youtube.com/watch?v=5LrVIablSJk&t=280s.

"User Experience (UX) is a catchy as well as tricky research topic, given its broad applications in a diversity of interactive systems and its deep root in various conceptual frameworks, for instance, psychological theories of emotion" [10]. Furthermore, Bernhaupt also highlights that UX in the iTV domain is related to four dimensions - aesthetics, emotion, stimulation and identification - measurable by a set of instruments, to assess non-instrumental and emotional reactions [11]. Also, ISO designates UX as: "A person's perceptions and responses that result from the use and/or anticipated use of a product, system or service" [12]. However, due to several possible ramifications, this definition originates more specific interpretations, such as: "User Experience explores how a person feels about using a product, i.e., the experiential, affective, meaningful and valuable aspects of product use" [13].

Regarding the UX process, the evaluation of a prototype by experts represents a crucial step towards the assessment of instrumental qualities related with a product's usability and a quick mean to gather relevant improvement suggestions. In this regard, two facts are important to highlight: (i) the evaluation of the UI should be as early as possible in order to offer designers the chance of getting feedback for the redesign process [14]; (ii) the selection of suitable evaluators considering their background, expertise and previous experience with similar systems [15]. After the definition of the experts, it is important to define methods and the tasks that will be applied [16].

Concerning the evaluation process with users on the TV ecosystem scenario, there are specificities that need to be considered before the realization of tests. The subjectivity of the user is a crucial factor to considerate, encompassing temporal, spatial, social, personal and technological factors, as well as the literacy level of each user. Simultaneously, many are the components that influence the UX in the iTV context, such as the Set-Top Box (STB) performance, the remote control, second-screen devices (smartphone and tablet), the television itself, among others contextual factors. Therefore, in the evaluation planning, is crucial to encompass usability questions, together with emotional factors as important topics to be assessed. Hence, it is necessary to use tools in order to comprise, not only instrumental qualities but others important aspects regarding the non-instrumental qualities of the UX [9, 17].

Among the several methods for usability evaluation, some of the most common are the heuristic evaluation, cognitive walkthrough and guideline review [16]. The think aloud protocol is also frequently used to encourage participants to express their opinions during the real-time experience. The heuristics consider a set of UI related principles. A cognitive walkthrough methodology is similar to a heuristic evaluation but with an emphasis on a task scenario that evaluators need to perform in the UI. The participants must go through predefined steps and identify issues concerning the interface and navigation. Finally, a guideline review involves having an evaluator comparing an interface against a detailed set of guidelines.

The experts' evaluation in the UltraTV project considered tasks converted to scenarios and contexts with specific navigational paths in order to create a guided interview for the evaluators, using a storyboard in a semi-functional prototype created on the Marvel platform accessed through an application provided by Apple TV. Additionally, in both, laboratory and experts' evaluations, the protocol comprised cognitive walkthrough and the think aloud methods.

On the second stage of the UltraTV assessment, the laboratory tests were focused on a triangulation of instruments [17] to collect feedback about the semi-functional prototype. For the perception of instrumental qualities (e.g. controllability, effectiveness, learnability), the SUS-System Usability Scale [18, 19] and the pragmatic dimension of the AttrakDiff were used. Regarding the evaluation of non-instrumental dimension, the hedonic dimension of AttrakDiff[7] (e.g. aesthetics, identification) was used; and, finally, to achieve emotional information reactions (e.g. satisfaction, motivation and control), the SAM-Self-Assessment Manikin [20] was the validated scale chosen to be applied in laboratory tests.

3 UltraTV Project: Prototype Development and Evaluation Methodology

The UltraTV project adopted an iterative and participatory design approach with the aim of developing a TV ecosystem that meets the contemporary demands regarding viewing habits and industry trends. The main goal is to consolidate an interactive TV ecosystem that supports the most innovative services while integrating audiovisual content (from different sources) in a unified way. In this sense, this project is focused on facilitating the access to On Demand content in an integrated UI, surpassing the linear and traditional organization of the channel's line-up. For this, it pursues the iterative design of user interfaces, as well as the validation of its feasibility through several testing methods (experts reviews, inLab tests and field trials). These goals have been translated into an UI proposal named TV Flow. The TV Flow aims to promote a consistent and fluid UX while interacting with an engaging interface, providing access to profile-based recommended content from different content sources. Additionally, the TV flow concept can be considered a different approach to zapping by promoting discovery of new contents, namely of content from players that the clients typically don't use, or, inversely, by promoting an easy access to frequently visited content sources, avoiding changing between different apps. With this aggregation and unification in mind, the UI intends to reconfigure the way people perceive and use the TV (see Table 2). Through a unified UI, content from different sources, namely from YouTube, Netflix, Facebook Videos along with traditional linear TV content is provided to the user. The content is laid out in a grid categorized in columns, according to genres (e.g. Sports, Information, Movies and Series) and sources (e.g. Live TV, YouTube, Facebook Videos, Netflix). The proposal of a disruptive UI for the unification of TV content aims precisely to enhance the entertainment experience offered to different consumer profiles – on the one hand by providing content beyond the traditional broadcast channels to the classic TV consumer (promoting the diversification of his choices), and on the other hand by aiming to capture the attention in TV content and improve the quality of OTT content viewing on the large TV screen for those who are used to watch videos using computer and mobile displays.

---

[7] AttrakDiff: http://attrakdiff.de/.

The initial tasks of the preliminary phase consisted in defining the requirements and guidelines of the intended solution. After the first sketches, low-fidelity mockups were created, tested and discussed internally by the different team members in brainstorming sessions. A medium fidelity prototype was then developed in the Sketch software, being later transposed to the Marvel application for the experts' review (see Table 2 – Version 1). The design of this first prototype was based on an exploratory interface supported on a grid-based navigation using the four remote control buttons and was then tested with the command belonging to the Apple TV (using the touch surface instead of the directional keys). As for as the prototype version tested inLab, it was developed using Luna, a JavaScript framework, installed in an Android box connected to the TV with a regular remote-control interaction (see Table 2 – Version 2).

The evaluation of the two versions of the prototype (Experts review for Version 1 and inLab tests for Version 2) were crucial to a better understanding of the system, namely to find how the prototype could be improved before its final assessment in a Field Trial.

3.1 Experts Review

In the UX evaluation process of preliminary prototypes, the expert's review represents a crucial step in the evaluation of a product and an agile method to gather relevant suggestions. For this to happen effectively two factors need to be taken into account: (i) UI assessment should be performed as early as possible to allow valid feedback for the redesign process; (ii) the selection of suitable evaluators considering their professional area and their experience with similar systems. Following the selection of experts, methods and tasks that effectively result in an overall analysis of the usability of the interface and the user experience should be provided.

For the UltraTV expert review [21], the analysis of users and tasks was converted to scenarios with specific navigational paths to create a cognitive walkthrough using a storyboard, allowing also free explorations whenever required. The session began with a presentation about the project and the evaluation objectives, complemented by a video that included transitions and animations of navigational menus, to give the evaluators a clear idea about the look & feel of the interface. During both the free explorations and the cognitive walkthrough of the prototype, the participants were encouraged to think aloud.

The UI assessment focused mainly on a qualitative approach to gather insights about navigation and graphical features to guide the redesign process. To complete this review efficiently, Nielsen's recommendation to use 5 experts was followed, since this number allows the identification of 85% of usability problems and was considered the most viable option for this qualitative test [22, 23].

3.2 Tests in Laboratory

Taking into consideration the recommendations obtained in the evaluation by experts and subsequent developments implemented in the system, the following objectives were defined for the tests with users in a laboratory environment (simulating a regular living room):

- determine the level of interest and acceptance of the overall proposal for unification of content from different sources based on user profiles;
- evaluate the intuition and consistency of the UI and navigation and grid-based organization;
- validate the keys of the remote control used to interact with the system;
- evaluate the overall appearance of the interface, including graphic aspects such as color, iconography, shapes and effects;
- determine the relevance of specific features (display modes, icons, profiles...);
- identify global and localized usability issues;
- gather information about users' needs and suggestions.

To achieve the established objectives, exploratory assessments (cognitive walk-through and think aloud) and validated usability and UX scales (SUS, SAM and AttrakDiff) were applied. Table 1 shows a concise description of each phase of the inLab tests.

Table 1. Activities carried in the tests of the UltraTV prototype.

Phases	Activity	Description
Introduction	Characterization Questionnaire	Focused on demographics, TV consumption habits and devices usage
	Project introduction	Introduction about the project and the structure of the test session
	Free exploration	Free exploration of the application for a few minutes
Exploration	Cognitive walkthrough	14 tasks mainly focused on navigation and features usage
	Exploration with think aloud	Free exploration of the application for a few minutes
Assessment	SUS (System Usability Scale)	Global usability overview using a ten-item attitude Likert scale
	SAM (Self-Assessment Manikin)	Non-verbal pictorial assessment that measures the satisfaction, motivation, and control associated with a person's affective reaction
	AttrakDiff	Instrumental and non-instrumental issues evaluation
	Interview	Interview including open-ended and close-ended questions

3.3 Participants Characterization

Regarding the expert's review, five evaluators were selected. Two experts with an academic background in technology, namely in UX and UI, being professors at the Illinois Institute of Technology of the Institute of Design- Chicago/USA; three experts developers of IPTV and iTV systems in Altice Labs (Portugal), with experience in UX and Human-Computer Interaction (HCI).

Regarding the inLab tests, a total of 20 participants took part in the tests sessions (10 males and 10 females), aged between 20 and 53 years old (average age = 28.5).

The sample consisted of individuals with different qualifications: Primary education (1), Secondary education (7), Bachelor's degree (7), Post-graduation (1), Master's degree (3) and PhD (1). Considering the professional occupation, it included: students (10); research fellows (5); employees (2): unemployed (1): retired (1): and freelancers (1). Regarding the TV consumption habits, 80% of the participants stated to have at least one television at home and to use a TV subscription service. Only 15% of participants referred not having access to any pay-TV service. Within the selected sample, the clear majority watched television at home (70%).

4   Results and Impacts on Prototype Development

For the presentation of the results the chronological order of the evaluations will be followed.

4.1   Results from the Experts' Review and Impacts on the Prototype

Considering the experts' evaluation, the analysis of the interface and corresponding navigation (visualization mode; menu and profile; organization and unified content) and of the look & feel (contextual menu|animations and transitions|) was carried by the 5 experts.

The experts agreed with some of the proposals shown, namely the concept of the grid, the need to focus on active content and the need to better emphasize the selected content. The experts also expressed positive feedback on profiling and contextual menus. However, some issues originated divergent opinions. An example was the relevance of the two viewing modes (Table 2 – a1 and b1), being mentioned as confusing by some experts and, contrarily, being valued by others as a feature of customization and discovery. Only one expert clearly rejected the wide view mode, stating that he would only use the zoom mode. Other experts said that they would switch between the two modes as they had a clear idea of what they would like to see using zoom mode (Table 2 – b1), or whether they were open to other possible options using wide mode (Table 2 – a1). In terms of the unification of content, the main functionality of this solution, it was approved by all.

Following the experts' comments, several adjustments to the prototype were defined and a new version (Version 2) was created as a synthesis of those comments. This was the version used in the following evaluation step, the inLab tests Table 2 presents the differences between the two versions of the prototype, comparing four main areas of the UI, namely the home screen grid in the wide visualization mode (Table 2 – A), the home screen grid in the zoom visualization mode (Table 2 – B), the full screen information menu at the bottom of the screen (Table 2 – C) and the contextual menu also in full screen (Table 2 – D). Issues concerning hierarchy and contrast were addressed in the home screen grid to reinforce the vertical reading of the columns.

The header from Version 1 (Table 2 – a1) was replaced in Version 2 (Table 2 – a2) by a blob shaped menu with a fluid and animated behavior when changing status. This menu allows shifting the view mode, the profile and to access the search feature. The labels that identify each category/column were given a different graphic treatment to

Table 2. Comparison of prototype versions (Version 1 and 2)

Prototype – Version 1 (Experts Review)	Prototype – Version 2 (inLab Tests)
(A) Home screen – Wide view	
(a1)	(a2)
(B) Home screen – Zoom view	
(b1)	(b2)
(C) Full screen – Bottom Contextual Menu	
(c1)	(c2)
(D) Full screen – Bottom Contextual Menu	
(d1)	(d2)

avoid being interpreted as a menu. Furthermore, fewer content cards were exhibited in the grid reinforcing the scale focus given to the selected card. The central column, that displays the active topic, was also emphasized using a more vivid color. The zoom view mode (b2) was simplified with a cleaner approach and the focus on the selected video was also improved being displayed in a larger size and with the category label overlaid (e.g. "Mix TV" label that refers to a group of suggestions from catchup TV). The contextual menus that provide additional information (C) and offer additional features to interact with the content (D) were also redesigned. The bottom contextual menu (c2) suffered minor changes mainly in color and opacity becoming less disruptive. Additionally, the functionalities menu (d2) was placed at the top of the screen, following the same blob shape and behavior of the home screen menu and including five options instead of four (restart, record, dislike, next content, more info). The experts mentioned that displaying the contextual menu at the centered with a darker texture over the content (d1) represented an unnecessary spotlight on this menu becoming a disruptive obstacle to the content viewing experience. Modifications to the UI, like the ones mentioned above, regarding graphic elements, textures, color, text styles, animations and navigation were extremely relevant to improve the overall UX and provide a distinctive look & feel to the system. Based on these results, a new UI (Table 2 – a2, b2, c2, d2) was adjusted to allow its integration into the subsequent prototype to be evaluated in laboratory.

4.2 Results from InLab Tests and Impacts on the Prototype

Regarding the inLab tests, in the Cognitive walkthrough session, the success rate (on 14 tasks) was classified between the parameters 1 "without problems" and 2 "with some difficulty", with the average of all participants being 1.5 (being 1 "without problems" and 5 "did not complete") which shows no significant problems with the use of the prototype.

Participants were then asked to answer to a triangulation of instruments for UX evaluation [11, 17], namely the scales SUS, AttrakDiff and SAM, whose overall results are shown in Table 3:

In terms of instrumental qualities, the prototype scored 83,63 in the SUS scale (ranging from 0 to 100) and 1.64 in the Pragmatic Dimension of AttrakDiff (ranging from −3 to 3). This score reflects the user's controllability, effectiveness and

Table 3. Application score according to the SUS, SAM and AttrakDiff instruments.

Instrumental qualities				Non-instrumental qualities			Emotional reactions	
SUS (0 to 100)	AttrakDiff (−3 to 3)			SAM (1 to 9)			AttrakDiff (−3 to 3)	
	PQ	HQ-S	HQ-I	Sat.	Mot.	S. of C.	ATT	
83.63	1.64	1.24	1.49	7.8	7.5	7.4	2.01	
UX Dimensions		Stimulation	Identification	Emotion			Aesthetics	

learnability regarding the system, revealing that in this test stage the prototype was already getting favorable results.

According to the SUS classification scale, see Fig. 1, the average value was 83.63 ("Good"), although very close to the classification considered "Excellent" (85.5), which confirms a high level in terms of system usability, since the minimum acceptable value starts in the second quartile, which corresponds to a score of 62.6.

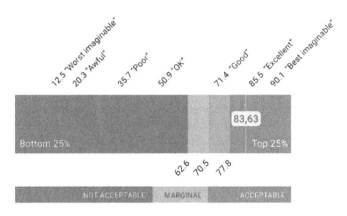

Fig. 1. Diagram with the prototype final score of SUS.

Regarding Self-Assessment Manikin (SAM) results, consolidating what was revealed in the SUS questionnaire, the participants demonstrated a positive emotional reaction in what concerns the use of the UltraTV prototype. The best scores were given to the satisfaction parameter, with an average of 7.80 in 9, and the motivation and control topics with nearly the same average, 7.55 and 7.45 respectively. Although in general good results was obtained, the need for improvements in the feeling of control over the application was detected, since the items related to this issue had lower scores. Similarly, it is necessary to remember that the tested prototype was not fully functional (although the grid interface was functional, users were shown areas with no possible interaction, which may have influenced the control quality).

Regarding the results obtained from the AttrakDiff scale, the average values of the 4 dimensions were calculated with all dimensions getting high scores (Fig. 2). Considering the instrumental aspects, the PQ obtained good values, following the usability results achieved by the SUS. However, the best results came from the Attractiveness (ATT) dimension, which is a non-instrumental quality and is strictly related to the aesthetic issues of the prototype. With an average value of 2.01, the value of the ATT dimension matches the qualitative feedback on the UI look & feel gathered in the interviews. In this same dimension, the results of the pairs of words "bad-good", "rejecting-inviting", and "disagreeable-likeable" were highlighted.

For non-instrumental dimensions, the HQ-I factor indicates the extent to which the system allows the user to identify with it, while the HQ-S dimension indicates originality, interest and encouragement towards the system. The HQ prototype scores in these dimensions (1.24 in HQ-S and 1.49 in HQ-I) show high rates of hedonic results, meaning

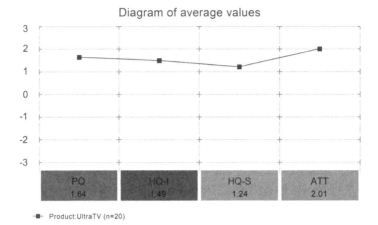

Fig. 2. The average values of the 4 AttrackDiff dimensions.

that the user identifies with the product, feels motivated and stimulated, and considers the product desirable (Fig. 3). In the HQ-I dimension, the "unpresentable - presentable" pair obtained the best result, while in the dimension HQ-S the pair "undemanding - challenging" was best classified. The AttrakDiff results, along with the scores obtained from

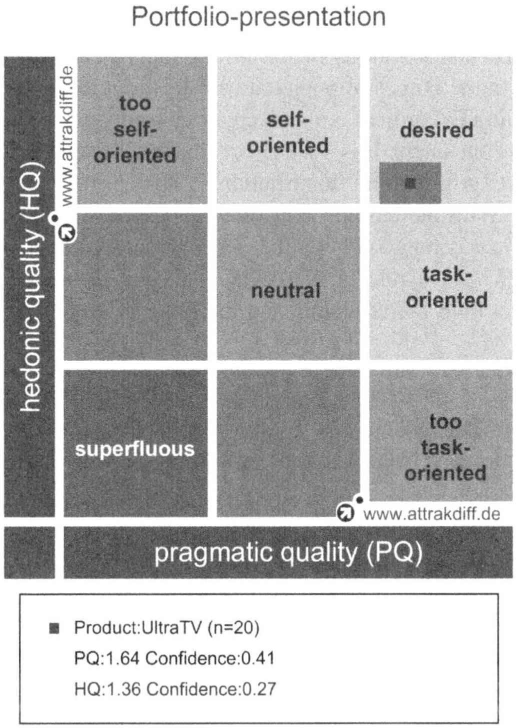

Portfolio-presentation

Fig. 3. Portfolio-presentation with confidence rectangles.

the SAM questionnaire, reveal that, although the participants consider the prototype undemanding, there are still problems in the manipulation of the system that can be subject to a more in-depth analysis using the users' feedback provided in the interviews.

Regarding this UI proposal, according to the inLab test evaluators the Version 2 of the prototype (Table 2 – a2, b2, c2, d2) was considered very thorough, intuitive and desirable, without being too complex. However, further recommendations were drawn from the inLab tests to be considered for an improved version to be used in the field trial (Version 3). Concerning the content unification, the need for the content to be hierarchized according to usage and consumption habits, placing at the top of the grid the more relevant content to the user, was identified. The results also showed the need for the search tool to be unified in a way that searches are global and related to all sources of content. Tutorials should be provided to elucidate about the structure and organization of the system. The need for a filtering system to simplify and customize the content presentation was also detected. Finally, concerning the customization of the system, the inclusion of a social component, like friends' recommendations was also mentioned.

5   Conclusions and Future Work

The preliminary evaluation made by the experts and later in the inLab tests allowed the team to gather a solid and highly relevant set of results crucial for the improvement and production of a functional prototype. The different results presented are contributing to the newer versions being developed. Subsequent to these evaluation stages, a proof of concept was achieved and iterations of the prototype are consolidating an improved version to be tested in the homes of potential users. Through this user centered design methodology, the UltraTV project aims to create a complete viewing ecosystem for television and video consumers. It is our believe that such conceptual development has the potential to make an important contribution to change the current television consumption paradigm. With the current and future evolutions, unified content and easy access to OTT sources, along with online social media content, we hope that the UltraTV project will have a role in the debate on what the future of the television system will be like at both the academic and the industry level.

Acknowledgments. This paper is a result of the UltraTV - UltraHD TV Application Ecosystem project (grant agreement no. 17738), funded by COMPETE 2020, Portugal 2020 and the European Union through the European Regional Development Fund (FEDER). Authors are grateful to the project partners: Altice Labs and Instituto de Telecomunicações.

References

1. Norman, D.A.: The Design of Everyday Things. Doubleday, New York (1990)
2. Interaction Design Foundation: The Basics of User Experience Design (2002)
3. Abreu, J., Almeida, P., Teles, B.: TV discovery & enjoy: a new approach to help users finding the right TV program to watch. In: Proceedings of the 2014 ACM International Conference on Interactive experiences for TV and online video, pp. 63–70. ACM (2014)

4. Vanattenhoven, J., Geerts, D.: Broadcast, video-on-demand, and other ways to watch television content: a household perspective. In: Proceedings of the 2015 ACM International Conference on Interactive Experiences for TV and Online Video, pp. 1–10. ACM (2015)
5. Vanattenhoven, J., Geerts, D.: Designing TV recommender interfaces for specific viewing experiences. In: Proceedings of the 2015 ACM International Conference on Interactive Experiences for TV and Online Video, pp. 185–190. ACM (2015)
6. Gonçalves, D., Costa, M., Couto, F.M.: A large-scale characterization of user behavior in cable TV. In: 3rd Workshop on Recommendation Systems for Television and Online Video (2016)
7. Abreu, J., Nogueira, J., Becker, V., Cardoso, B.: Survey of Catch-Up TV and other time-shift services: a comprehensive analysis and taxonomy of linear and nonlinear television. Telecommun. Syst. **64**, 57–74 (2017)
8. Cardoso, B., de Carvalho, F.: Trends in TV: OTT, Apps, Ads. Homepage http://www.alticelabs.com/content/07_TV.pdf. Accessed 22 Nov 2017
9. Hassenzahl, M., Tractinsky, N.: User experience - a research agenda. Behav. Inf. Technol. **25**, 91–97 (2006)
10. Law, E.L.-C.: The measurability and predictability of user experience. In: Proceedings of the 3rd ACM SIGCHI Symposium on Engineering Interactive Computing Systems - EICS 2011 (2011)
11. Bernhaupt, R., Pirker, M.: Evaluating user experience for interactive television: towards the development of a domain-specific user experience questionnaire. In: Kotzé, P., Marsden, G., Lindgaard, G., Wesson, J., Winckler, M. (eds.) INTERACT 2013. LNCS, vol. 8118, pp. 642–659. Springer, Heidelberg (2013). https://doi.org/10.1007/978-3-642-40480-1_45
12. ISO 9241-210, Ergonomics of Human–System Interaction – Part 210: Humancentred Design for Interactive Systems (2010)
13. User Experience (n.d.). https://en.wikipedia.org/wiki/User_experience. Accessed 22 Nov 2017
14. Demetriadis, S., Karoulis, A., Pombortsis, A.: "Graphical" Jogthrough: expert based methodology for user interface evaluation, applied in the case of an educational simulation interface. Comput. Educ. **32**, 285–299 (1999)
15. Jin, J., Geng, Q., Zhao, Q., Zhang, L.: Integrating the trend of research interest for reviewer assignment. In: International WWW Conference, pp. 1233–1241 (2017)
16. Rohrer, C.P., Boyle, F., Wendt, J., Sauro, J., Cole, S.: Practical usability ratings by experts: a pragmatic approach for scoring product usability. In: CHI 2016, vol. 38, pp. 333–358 (2016)
17. Abreu, J., Almeida, P., Silva, T.: A UX evaluation approach for second-screen applications. In: Abásolo, M., Perales, F., Bibiloni, A. (eds.) Applications and Usability of Interactive TV, vol. 605, pp. 105–120. Springer, Cham (2016)
18. Brooke, J.: SUS-A quick and dirty usability scale. In: Jordan, P.W., Weerdmeester, P.W., Thomas, P.W., McLelland, I.L. (eds.) Usability Evaluation in Industry, pp. 189–194. Taylor and Francis, London (2015)
19. Martins, A., Rosa, A., Queirós, A., Silva, A., Rocha, N.P.: European Portuguese validation of the usability scale (SUS). In: 6th International Conference on Software Development and Technologies for Enhancing, pp. 293–300 (1996, 2015)
20. Bradley, M.M., Lang, P.J.: Measuring emotion: the self-assessment manikin and the semantic differential. J. Behav. Ther. Exper. Psychiatry **25**(1), 49–59 (1994)
21. Almeida, P., Abreu, J., Oliveira, E., Velhinho, A.: Proceedings of 6th Iberoamerican Conference on Applications and Usability for Interactive TV, pp. 59–70. University of Aveiro, Aveiro, Portugal (2017)
22. Nielsen, J.: Why You Only Need to Test with 5 Users (2000). https://www.nngroup.com/articles/why-you-only-need-to-test-with-5-users/. Accessed 22 Nov 2017
23. Nielsen, J.: How Many Test Users in a Usability Study? https://www.nngroup.com/articles/how-many-test-users/. Accessed 22 Nov 2012

IDTV Content Recommendation

Machine Learning the TV Consumption:
A Basis for a Recommendation System

Bernardo Cardoso[✉] and Jorge Abreu

University of Aveiro, Aveiro, Portugal
{bernardoc,jfa}@ua.pt

Abstract. With the continuous growth of channels and content available in a typical interactive TV service, viewers have become increasingly frustrated, struggling to select which programs to watch. Content recommendation systems have been pointed out as a possible tool to mitigate this problem, especially when applied to on-demand content. However, in linear content, its success has been limited, either due to the specificities of this type of content or due to the little integration with normal consumption behaviors. Despite that, recommendation algorithms have undergone a set of enhancements in order to improve their effectiveness, particularly when applied to the world of linear content. These improvements, focused on the use of the visualization context, paired with machine learning techniques, can represent a big advantage in the quality of the suggestions to be proposed to the viewer. The area of user experience (UX) evaluation, in interactive TV, has been also a subject of ongoing research, extending beyond the traditional usability evaluation, pursuing other dimensions of analysis such as identification, emotion, stimulation, and aesthetics, as well as distinct moments of evaluation. This paper presents the proposal for the development of a recommendation system, based on the viewing context, and a methodology for evaluating the way this system influences the UX of the viewers.

Keywords: TV · UX evaluation · Recommendations · Visualization context

1 Introduction

In the last decades, the quantity and quality of the content available in a typical living room have increased considerably. Television, the main distributor of this content had, concurrently, a clear evolution. Not only have the number of available channels improved significantly, particularly on paid TV platforms and in more developed countries, but also, as a result of digitalization and interactivity, a number of additional features have appeared, granting a considerable increase on the available content. These new functionalities include, for example, video on demand (VOD), automated catch-up TV, digital video recorder (DVR), and over-the-top (OTT) media services like Netflix and Hulu, which can be classified in a taxonomy that distinguishes between linear content, i.e., traditional television, transmitted in broadcast mode and nonlinear content, which include services that provide movies and television programs by request [1].

© Springer International Publishing AG, part of Springer Nature 2018
M. J. Abásolo et al. (Eds.): jAUTI 2017, CCIS 813, pp. 61–74, 2018.
https://doi.org/10.1007/978-3-319-90170-1_5

All this increase in content and functionality can add up really quick, resulting in a much wider choice for the end users. Accompanying this, there is also a progressive complexification on the interaction modes. In one hand, the amount of content is so great that the viewer has difficulty in selecting a proper program to see, attaining a so-called "Paradox of Choice" [2, 3]. On the other hand, the tools that could help him in this task are of limited practical use, partly because of the physical limitations of the equipment itself (the user is too far away from the screen to be able to discern very detailed elements) and also because he interacts through a remote control with limited interaction features, which are not always adapted to the new interactive TV services [4].

This paper will focus on a proposal to develop and evaluate the user experience of an interactive TV application, dubbed TV Concierge, that aims to mitigate this paradox of choice, by artificially reducing the quantity of content presented at each moment to the user, through the use of personalization and, at the same time, building a minimalist user interface that further limits the number of interactions needed. In this way, in Sect. 2 we address a set of recently researched recommendation algorithms and techniques that rely on the TV consumption context and can be applied to linear TV content. In Sect. 3 we present the way we conceive the use of machine learning in the implementation of the recommender system. Then, in Sect. 4 we provide the results of our initial data analysis and also a visualization for a sampling of this data. In Sect. 5 we address the development of the correspondent interactive TV application and some of the mockups already designed. Next, on Sect. 6 we describe our user experience evaluation methodology and how we envisage executing it. Finally, in Sect. 7 the paper is wrapped up with the exposition of the results we expect to achieve in the upcoming months and some brief conclusions.

2   Personalization and Recommendations in Linear TV

In order to mitigate the nuisances caused by the content proliferation and a situation where the user expends a lot of time looking for content to watch (for instance, Digitalsmiths reports that 45.7% of respondents spend 5–20 min per day channel surfing [5]), several proposals have been made, most of them focusing on the use of recommendation and personalization systems, in order to facilitate the discovery of interesting content to watch [6]. These systems have achieved effective success in on-demand video subscription platforms such as Netflix and the traditional VOD platforms of the various pay-TV operators, where there is a significant control over the offer of content to recommend and where the user is already predisposed to a more advanced level of interaction, namely with a greater propensity to assign scores to the viewed content. However, in linear content, recommendations are still not an effective tool [6] and end up being just another functionality, lost among many others and far from being a solution that truly contributes to an effective mitigation of the problem [7].

Some particularities of linear content add greater complexity in creating an effective recommendation system, namely the content catalog being in constant change and the content being available only for a short time due to the TV channels programming being characterized by its constant renewal [6]. A recommendation system, that only has access to the linear channels programming, can only recommend, at any moment, the programs that these channels are broadcasting or programs that will start in the upcoming minutes. Even systems that have access to a catch-up TV catalog, need to deal with the fact that fresh content is entering the collection all the time, since the system is constantly recording new programs and, similarly, removing older ones [1]. In contrast, VOD recommendation systems do not need to take these factors into account, as their catalogs have much slower turnover cycles.

Another characteristic of linear TV consumption that should be emphasized is that it normally follows a very regular pattern [6]. Contrary to a VOD system where the viewer usually wants to find a new movie to watch, when watching TV the consumer has habits associated with certain times of the day and follows specific recurring programs on a small number of available channels [5]. This regularity together with other contextual aspects of TV watching was also identified by other authors [3, 8, 9], who take them as the basis for proposing new approaches in recommending linear television content.

In [3], the authors looked for a better understanding of the contextual aspects involved in TV and video consumption on a domestic environment through the execution of two ethnographic studies. In the first, which involved 12 households, they observed how the household structure determines the viewing situations and the relations between the amount of attention, type of content and viewing behavior – planned, routine, or spontaneous. They also observed the different ways in which people discover new content. In a second, multi-method study, comprising 7 families with children, typical situations of visualization and their contextual aspects were assessed. After combining the results of both studies, they recognized seven viewing situations: weekend mornings; when the children are sleeping; family quality time; relaxing after school; a free moment: men and sports; and lazy afternoons. In each case they identified the contextual aspects: mood; content; viewers; time; content delivery time (linear or on-demand); and viewing mode (attention level associated with consumption). With the results of these studies, they make several proposals for recommendation systems, algorithms and user interface designs that could take into account these contextual aspects. Unfortunately, some of these contextual aspects are not easily assessed in an automated way, mood and viewing mode for instance, and cannot be used as-is in a non-intrusive solution.

Other authors found out that linear TV consumption patterns are strongly conditioned by time context and channel preferences [6]. In this sense, they propose that one way to go beyond the state of the art on the current recommendation systems for linear content is to explore and integrate this visualization context (time) in the user consumption modeling. Through empirical evaluation with a broad set of linear TV data, they demonstrate a significant improvement in the quality of the recommendations when the time context is taken into account. This usage of time context can be improved with the addition of implicit feedback, taken from consumer data analysis, and taking into account not only the linear TV services, but also the catalog of catch-up TV available today from most operators. Comparing this approach with current algorithms it has been shown it can be superior to these in accuracy, while maintaining good levels of diversity and serendipity [9].

In addition to the temporal context, an attractive idea, that has been shown to provide considerable precision gains in the recommendations, is the usage of a sequential context [8], which takes into account the last viewed program at the time of the recommendation to influence it.

An important aspect of TV consumption is that it is often shared by several different users, whose tastes can vary widely. Typical recommendation systems do not handle this situation very well, since visualization data is typically collected and modeled at the device level, aggregating all users and obscuring their individual tastes. The ideal contextual information would be for the system to know in each moment who is watching and their level of attention. That level of information is hard to attain today, without the introduction of additional hardware in the living room. A further layer of additional contextual information, that can be obtained automatically, must still be devised to mitigate this issue.

3   Technical Approach

Most recommender systems fall into two basic types: collaborative filtering and content-based filtering. In the first, a profile of a user is built with information from past behavior, i.e., books or movies purchased or ratings given. Thereafter, this model is used for comparison with models from other users, looking for similar profiles. The new/different items are then used as recommendations. Content-based filtering, on the other way, uses intrinsic characteristics of the items, like subject, color or length to find similarities between items, and use the related outcomes as recommendations. The difference between these two basic types can be demonstrated in an online bookstore like Amazon: collaborative filtering produces recommendations like "Customer that purchased this book also purchased these and these" and content-based filtering generate suggestions like "Books similar to this one are x and y". These approaches are often combined in so-called hybrid recommender systems [10].

These standard approaches focus on the most relevant items to recommend to a user but do not take into consideration any contextual information, such as time, place, and the company of other people. They just deal with two basic types of entities - users and items - not putting them into a context when providing recommendations.

However, as we presented in the last section, context can be a fundamental entity for personalization in linear TV. Context can also impact situations already tackled by common approaches, for example, the rating a viewer gives to a movie also depends on where and how he viewed the movie, at what time, and with whom. Also, the type of movie a person recommends to a colleague will differ significantly depending on whether he is going to see it on a Monday with his parents or on a Friday night with his girlfriend [11]. This awareness leveraged the introduction of context-aware recommendation capabilities in different applications (namely in mobile platforms where location information provided by GPS has a huge impact on the acuity of the recommendations) and the development of a new research area, related to context-aware recommendation systems. For example, in [11], a notion of context is presented along with how it can be modeled in recommender systems. The major approaches to modeling contextual information are also discussed through three main algorithmic paradigms: contextual pre-filtering, post-filtering, and modeling. The TV Concierge interactive application will make good of this research and will apply it to the recommender system being developed.

At this moment, the technical approach for the development of the recommender system is to base it on decision trees, one of the most used building blocks in current machine learning approaches. The choosing of decision trees for the building of the recommendation system was based on several benefits they offer: efficiency, interpretability, and flexibility in handling a variety of input data types (ratings, demographic, contextual, etc.) [12].

Decision trees are a very simple notion. At the core, they are nothing more than a cascade of if-then-else(s). Using the tree concept, the nodes represent questions, being the leafs the final decisions. Materializing a little the concept within the TV Concierge interactive application, the questions could be like "Is today a weekday?", "Is the current time noon?", "Was the previously watched channel MTV?", and so on. A sample tree like this can be seen in Fig. 1. After answering the sequence of questions, the system will reach a leaf where there will be one or more TV programs that will be used as the recommendations.

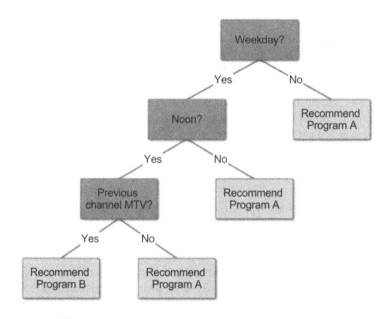

Fig. 1. Sample decision tree for program recommendation

Efficiency is very important because the system will need to create a personalized recommender system for each individual STB, and will use real-time data like the previously watched program or the current time of day as the basic input to generate a recommendation. In this framework, it needs to be very efficient to be able to generate a new program recommendation in a timely fashion. Decision trees, being a simple cascade of if-then-else(s), are very fast to use and relatively easy to construct.

Interpretability is a real plus in the TV Concierge interactive application because in some of the current recommendation systems, namely the ones based on neural networks, is very difficult to understand how the system arrived at some recommendation [10]. In the case of decision trees, interpreting the result is as simple as backtracking the tree and at each node evaluating what was the deciding attribute.

Finally, the capability to handle a lot of different data types is also a must, because TV Concierge will need to process different things like time-of-day, day-of-week, current channel, previous program, etc.

Obviously, decision trees can be written by hand, in an ad hoc way, actually, that is what most computer programmers do most of the time, since a computer program is a decision tree with some additional concepts on top of it. The use of machine learning allows for the computer to essentially write the program itself, based on the recollected usage data, in this case, from each STB. There are different algorithms to construct decision trees from a dataset, but the main idea is to uncover the most significant attribute within the data (the one with most information gain) and root the tree with it. Then, iteratively repeat the process with the remaining unused attributes, until there are no more attributes or all the elements are indistinguishable, at which point the identified items are converted in leafs representing the decision [13].

The advantages of having the computer automatically generate the decision trees are evident, since it allows each and every STB to have a personalized recommender (the decision tree), but also because sometimes the machine learning approach reveals hidden associations in the data that are not easily perceived at first sight.

The main limitation of this approach is the so-called "cold start" problem. This kind of recommender, based on historical data, is incapable of providing any recommendation until a minimum dataset is gathered. How to overcome this issue in TV Concierge is still being researched at the moment.

4   Initial Data Analysis

In the preparation for this proposal, to partially validate our assumptions and techno-logical approaches, we have been collecting usage logs from a set of consenting users on a commercial IPTV platform (based on Ericsson Mediaroom [14]). This allowed us to understand the challenges associated with processing these events, which in real life are very noisy and need a lot of work before being in a way that can be used in a practical way. The same challenges have been found before with the same platform [15] and we resort to some of the same solutions in the pre-processing of the data, like only taking in account visualization events that spanned more than 5 min or preemptively ending watching periods that took more than 4 h without any user interaction.

However, our main interest in this initial data analysis was to find out if there were indeed easily identifiable patterns within the television usage of real users. For that, and because patterns are more easily spotted visually than analytically, we took one month of usage events from the STBs and plotted them in an agenda like view, grouping the events by day of the week (e.g. all the views of the different Mondays where grouped in a line title Monday, etc.). The events were also color-coded by channel and titled with the channel name and the viewing mode (live, catchup, VOD, DVR, etc.). An example plotting for two weekdays can be seen in Fig. 2. In the full plot we can also see that weekdays are much more regular than weekends. It is also noticeable that the period from 20:00 to 0:00 is where there is more turbulence. Despite that, in this example, the timeslot from late-night crossing Monday to Tuesday is very regular.

Fig. 2. Mondays and Tuesday events for one STB through the period of one month (Color figure online)

This was in line with our expectations and we found that there are indeed relevant patterns in the watching data, and even if the patterns are less evident in the primetime timeslot (the most prized time in TV) this was also anticipated, representing perhaps a lot of channel surfing and the endless pursuit of content that TV Concierge aims to mitigate. We also expect that the machine learning algorithms will catch some of the hidden, but latent, patterns still present in the data.

Anyhow, we assume that the introduction of the TV Concierge interactive application, if successful, can mitigate appreciably this turbulence. This will be actually one of the ways in which we could validate the impact of the TV Concierge, by comparing the variability of watched programs before and after the introduction of the system.

5   Prototype Design

With new recommendation algorithms, that take into account diversified contextual aspects of TV consumption, that are more focused on linear content problems, we have the foundations to the most important backend component of the TV Concierge interactive application. However, the introduction of these features cannot be dissociated from the way the viewer can access it. It is important to note that, although there is a significant research specifically regarding interfaces to interactive TV recommendations systems, some authors report that many users preferred to have few or no interactions with the system [16]. Nevertheless, current implementations rely mainly on solutions where the recommendation is only realized after some kind of user activity [17, 18], sometimes forcing the response to a series of questions before any recommendation can be made.

This mismatch between the user expectations and the way the features are implemented shows that the relationship between the viewer and the TV goes far beyond the user interface, covering a set of other dimensions in what can be called, generally, the user experience (UX). In the ISO 9241-210 standard, UX is considered as the "person's perceptions and responses resulting from the use and/or anticipated use of a product, system or service" [19]. In the notes associated with this definition, this standardization body stresses that UX includes all the emotions, beliefs, preferences, perceptions, physical and psychological responses, behaviors and achievements associated with the user, whether they occur before, during or after use.

In "The Paradox of Choice: Why More Is Less" [2], the psychologist Barry Schwartz, explains why a lot of choices can be detrimental to people's psychological and emotional well-being. It explains how a culture that grows with an infinite availability of constantly evolving options can also foster deep dissatisfaction, which can lead to paralysis in decision making and, in some cases, depression. It also describes the difficulty of choosing a program to view when there are so many available, and that in this sense the (traditional) recommendations systems still make the situation worse, since they always propose something new, never seen.

Combining these insights, our prototype design took an approach that tries to minimize the number of interactions the user needs to perform with the system. Simultaneously we aim to bring the recommendations to the upfront of the platform – in this respect, the system will not just wait for the user to ask for some recommendation but will preemptively suggest them. This will start from the very beginning, i.e., when the user turns on its Set-top Box (STB) it will be presented with the program that makes sense to play at the time it is turning the box on, rather than with the last channel tuned in the previous night. In addition, making use of the time-shifting capabilities of modern TV platforms, the suggested program will start from the beginning. For instance, if a potential viewer, who usually watches the TV newscast when he gets home about 8:00 pm, turns on the STB around this time, the recommendation system will automatically start playing the newscast that the viewer usually sees and not a spurious channel, kept from the last viewing session. This use case is illustrated in the left side of Fig. 3.

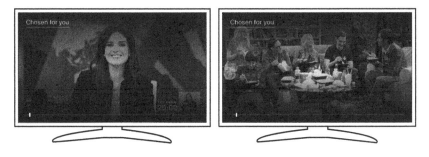

Fig. 3. Mockup for the automatic program suggestion

It is also intended that when a program finishes and whenever the system has a high degree of confidence, it will automatically start playing the next suggestion, without any intervention from the viewer. This situation is illustrated in the right side of Fig. 3 – at the end of the newscast the system suggested an episode from a series and began its reproduction automatically, from the beginning.

When the system does not have a sufficient degree of confidence, it will select a reduced number of proposals for the viewer. In this case, the playback will still start automatically, but the viewer will get, for a few seconds, the opportunity to choose another program to watch, a concept that is visible in Fig. 4, mimicking a typical binge-watching scenario [20], which is somewhat the brand mark of the current OTT video-on-demand systems from the internet.

It is also possible that the system has no suggestion to propose at a certain time, for example when no pattern has been identified, in this case, the system needs to propose a new program. Our approach to this situation is that the system will suggest a new release (e.g. a new season of a TV series) between a limited set of the most watched channels on that STB. The idea behind this methodology is that, usually, if a series that a viewer normally watches has ended, a new one will be released to take its timeslot, and the system will offer that. If that does not happen, some other channel that the viewer also watches will have something starting to promote. We already know that the user likes the channel, so there is a higher probability that it also likes a new show from that channel. This is the purpose of the interface shown on the right side of Fig. 4 – in this case, we opted for the binge-watching interface for the user to have an opportunity to actually select the new program.

Although the interactive application will start automatically when the STB is turned on, and will keep providing suggestions and playing content in an automated way, this does not mean that the user relinquishes all the control of the STB. The user can, at any moment, use his interactive TV system as usual and TV Concierge will disappear. It can be summoned again by the standard means of the interactive platform, for instance with a menu item or from a dedicated button in the remote, but it will also restart offering suggestions automatically if it detects that a program the viewer is watching just ended or upon detection of what we call a "mindless zapping", that is, when the user starts zapping in a pattern that appears to be just hunting for something to watch.

Fig. 4. Mockup of the system allowing the selection of the following suggestion

6   UX Evaluation

As stated in the introduction, one of the key aims of the TV Concierge interactive application is to evaluate the way that an interactive TV recommendation system, based on the viewing context as described in the previous section, influences the UX of its viewers. To achieve this objective, we will address several dimensions of the UX, namely: usability, aesthetic, emotional, stimulation and identification, through the use of a methodology based on a framework that uses previously endorsed and validated tools [21], and is highly aligned with some previous similar evaluations [22, 23].

In our context of evaluation, the usability dimension can be understood "as being a general quality of the appropriateness to a purpose of any particular artefact" [24]. The aesthetics dimension portrays how visually pleasing or beautiful something is perceived. The emotion dimension portrays the emotional response to the outcome of the interaction with the product or service. The stimulation dimension describes the way a product addresses the human necessity for innovative and interesting functions, interactions and content. Finally, the identification dimension indicates how a certain product allows the user to identify himself with it, by using or owning a specific product the user can reach a chosen self-presentation [22].

This framework proposes different tools for each of the distinct UX dimensions. Thus, for the usability/pragmatic dimension, the System Usability Scale (SUS) [24] will be used. This is a questionnaire with 10 items on a five-point Likert scale, which presents a final result in a range between 0 and 100. For this dimension, we will also use Pragmatic Quality (QP) component of the AttrakDiff questionnaire [25, 26]. Each of the AttrakDiff components has a value between -3 and 3 and represents an average of 7 items on a semantic differential scale of bipolar adjectives. For the aesthetics dimension, we will use the AttrakDiff Attractiveness component.

For the emotional dimension, the pictorial assessment tool Self-Assessment Manikin (SAM) [27] will be considered in its 3 indicators: pleasure, arousal, and dominance. This non-verbal tool measures the results for each of the indicators on a scale from 1 to 9. For the stimulation and identification dimensions, the corresponding AttrakDiff Hedonic Quality (HQ-S and HQ-I) components will be used.

To better understand the model that we intended to use for the operationalization of the research project, it is important to point out that the UX does not happen in a single instant, in reality, it happens in a set of distinct and conjugated moments. Thus, even before the user comes into contact with a new product or service he already has the experience of using other solutions, similar or not. When he receives information about a new system, it creates a set of expectations and a mental model of how it will work, in what Roto et al. call of anticipated UX [28]. In the first experience with the system and with every additional interaction, there are moments of what these authors call momentary UX, i.e. UX experienced, sometimes viscerally, during use. After a usage session and reflecting on it, the user achieves the called episodic UX that recovers the memory of the sensations and emotions he had during that previous use. Over time and after several periods of use (interleaved by times of non-use), a cumulative UX is reached where the various individual experiences merge to create a whole experience, which may be the most important. As

Roto et al. refer, the importance of a negative reaction during a specific use can be diminished by successive subsequent uses and the problematic use can be, in the end, remembered differently. Each of these different UX moments will be carefully studied using different tools. To address the anticipated UX, we intend to use semi-structured interviews, which will be carried out with a limited set of experts and end users. For the evaluation of the momentary UX, the ideal methodology would be direct observation, in order to capture the behaviors at the precise moment they occur. However, since the normal usage will occur in a residential environment by a large number of viewers simultaneously, this would be impractical. The alternative that this research intends to implement is the well-timed use of in-app questions, which will be presented to the viewer directly on the TV, in a way similar to the one depicted in Fig. 5. The use of this approach will also allow for the evaluation of the suggestions system since the experienced results are easily transformable in simple questions, with a very direct response from the viewer, and can be very tuned to the respective functionalities.

Fig. 5. Mockup of an in-app question being made directly on the TV

The assessment of the episodic UX will be realized carried out shortly after the installation of the prototype and will be performed in an internet application using the three instruments previously mentioned SUS, SAM and AttrakDiff, instructing the viewer that he should respond by recalling the most recent prototype usage. The evaluation of the cumulative UX, which will use the same three instruments, will be applied in the same way, three months after the system setup, along with a semi-structured interview.

The data collected by these instruments will be tabulated and compared to understand the evolution of the UX perception towards the system. A set of indicators will be collected automatically by the interactive TV platform, to serve as a control and as a potential triangulation of the information collected in the questionnaires. This will allow us to better evaluate scenarios where the user reports that he strongly agrees to "I think that I would like to use this system frequently", the first question in SUS, and then seldom using the system.

7   Expected Results

With the insights obtained through the data analysis, we expect to achieve a rich under-standing of the influence that a recommendation system, based on the viewing context, and relying on machine learning techniques, has on the UX of the viewers. Furthermore, we will also assess the relationship between the reduction of the number of content options offered to the viewer and their respective UX. As already mentioned, the exces-sive content can become a source of frustration for the viewer. Following this reasoning, we expect that reducing the number of options will lessen this frustration [2]. We also intend to evaluate the usage of in-app questions, directly on the interactive TV interface, in the UX evaluation context. This inquiring model has a set of advantages, since it enables a real continuity between the moment of UX and the moment of the evaluation and allows an automatic data collection. However, it interferes directly with the inter-action flow which in itself will change the perceived UX [29].

The enormous growth in content available in most pay-TV platforms has the poten-tial for creating a "Paradox of Choice" in the viewer. Taking advantage of new devel-opments in recommendation algorithms, based on the viewing context and much more tailored to linear content, we propose to implement a recommendation system using machine learning and apply this recommendations on a preemptive interactive TV application that will act upon these recommendations and actually plays automatically the content, minimizing the viewer interactions and decisions. From the initial data analysis, we have already found that there is an effective regularity in the sampled TV usage, and that it can be leveraged into the creation of the proposed robot concierge. We need now to evaluate how such a system can affect the UX of its viewers, to get a real understanding of its potential in the linear content context.

References

1. Abreu, J., Nogueira, J., Becker, V., Cardoso, B.: Survey of Catch-up TV and other time-shift services: a comprehensive analysis and taxonomy of linear and nonlinear television. Telecommun. Syst. **64**, 57–74 (2017). https://doi.org/10.1007/s11235-016-0157-3
2. Schwartz, B.: The Paradox of Choice: Why More is Less. HarperCollins, New York City (2004)
3. Vanattenhoven, J., Geerts, D.: Contextual aspects of typical viewing situations: a new perspective for recommending television and video content. Pers. Ubiquit. Comput. **19**, 761–779 (2015). https://doi.org/10.1007/s00779-015-0861-0
4. Bernhaupt, R., Obrist, M., Weiss, A., et al.: Trends in the living room and beyond: results from ethnographic studies using creative and playful probing. Comput. Entertain. **6**, 5:1–5:23 (2008). https://doi.org/10.1145/1350843.1350848
5. Digitalsmiths: Q4 2015 Video Trends Report - Consumer Behavior Across Pay-TV, VOD, PPV, OTT, TVE, Connected Devices, and Content Discovery (2015)
6. Turrin, R., Condorelli, A., Cremonesi, P., Pagano, R.: Time-based TV programs prediction. In: 1st Workshop on Recommender Systems for Television and Online Video at ACM RecSys (2014)
7. Churchill, E.F.: Putting the person back into personalization. Interactions **20**, 12–15 (2013). https://doi.org/10.1145/2504847

8. Aharon, M., Hillel, E., Kagian, A., Lempel, R., Makabee, H., Nissim, R.: Watch-it-next: a contextual TV recommendation system. In: Bifet, A., May, M., Zadrozny, B., Gavalda, R., Pedreschi, D., Bonchi, F., Cardoso, J., Spiliopoulou, M. (eds.) ECML PKDD 2015. LNCS (LNAI), vol. 9286, pp. 180–195. Springer, Cham (2015). https://doi.org/10.1007/978-3-319-23461-8_12

9. Gonçalves, D., Costa, M., Couto, F.M.: A flexible recommendation system for cable TV. In: 3rd Workshop on Recommendation Systems for Television and online Video, RecSysTV 2016 (2016)

10. Portugal, I., Alencar, P., Cowan, D.: The use of machine learning algorithms in recommender systems: a systematic review. Expert Syst. Appl. **97**, 205–227 (2018). https://doi.org/10.1016/j.eswa.2017.12.020

11. Adomavicius, G., Tuzhilin, A.: Context-aware recommender systems. In: Ricci, F., Rokach, L., Shapira, B. (eds.) Recommender Systems Handbook, pp. 191–226. Springer, Boston (2015). https://doi.org/10.1007/978-1-4899-7637-6_6

12. Zhang, T., Iyengar, V.S.: Recommender systems using linear classifiers. J. Mach. Learn. Res. **2**, 313–334 (2002)

13. Quinlan, J.R.: Induction of decision trees. Mach. Learn. **1**, 81–106 (1986). https://doi.org/10.1023/A:1022643204877

14. Ericsson AB Mediaroom—Ericsson Media Solutions. https://mediasolutions.ericsson.com/products/mediaroom/. Accessed 8 Jan 2018

15. Zibriczky, D., Petres, Z., Waszlavik, M., Tikk, D.: EPG content recommendation in large scale: a case study on interactive TV platform. In: 2013 12th International Conference on Machine Learning and Applications, pp. 315–320 (2013)

16. Buczak, A.L., Zimmerman, J., Kurapati, K.: Personalization: improving ease-of-use, trust and accuracy of a TV show recommender. In: Proceedings of AH 2002 Workshop on Personalization in Future TV (2002)

17. Chang, N., Irvan, M., Terano, T.: A TV program recommender framework. Proc. Comput. Sci. **22**, 561–570 (2013). https://doi.org/10.1016/j.procs.2013.09.136

18. Swearingen, K., Sinha, R.: Interaction design for recommender systems. Des. Interact. Syst. **6**, 312–334 (2002)

19. International Organization for Standardization: ISO 9241-210: ergonomics of human–system interaction - human-centred design for interactive systems. Int. Organ. Stand. **2010**, 32 (2010). https://doi.org/10.1039/c0dt90114h

20. Jenner, M.: Binge-watching: video-on-demand, quality TV and mainstreaming fandom. Int. J. Cult. Stud. **20**, 304–320 (2017). https://doi.org/10.1177/1367877915606485

21. Abreu, J., Almeida, P., Silva, T.: A UX evaluation approach for second-screen applications. Commun. Comput. Inf. Sci. **605**, 105–120 (2016). https://doi.org/10.1007/978-3-319-38907-3_9

22. Bernhaupt, R., Pirker, M.: Evaluating user experience for interactive television: towards the development of a domain-specific user experience questionnaire. In: Kotzé, P., Marsden, G., Lindgaard, G., Wesson, J., Winckler, M. (eds.) INTERACT 2013. LNCS, vol. 8118, pp. 642–659. Springer, Heidelberg (2013). https://doi.org/10.1007/978-3-642-40480-1_45

23. Drouet, D., Bernhaupt, R.: User experience evaluation methods: lessons learned from an interactive TV case-study. In: Bogdan, C., et al. (eds.) HCSE/HESSD -2016. LNCS, vol. 9856, pp. 351–358. Springer, Cham (2016). https://doi.org/10.1007/978-3-319-44902-9_22

24. Brooke, J.: SUS-a quick and dirty usability scale. Usability Eval. Ind. **189**, 4–7 (1996)

25. Hassenzahl, M., Burmester, M., Koller, F.: AttrakDiff: Ein Fragebogen zur Messung wahrgenommener hedonischer und pragmatischer Qualität. In: Szwillus, G., Ziegler, J. (eds.) 2003 Interaktion Bewegung Mensch & Computer, pp. 187–196. Vieweg + Teubner Verlag, Wiesbaden (2003)
26. Hassenzahl, M.: The interplay of beauty, goodness, and usability in interactive products. Hum.-Comput. Interact. **19**, 319–349 (2008). https://doi.org/10.1207/s15327051hci1904_2
27. Bradley, M.M., Lang, P.J.: Measuring emotion: the self-assessment manikin and the semantic differential. J. Behav. Ther. Exp. Psychiatry **25**, 49–59 (1994). https://doi.org/10.1016/0005-7916(94)90063-9
28. Roto, V., Law, E., Vermeeren, A., Hoonhout, J.: User experience white paper. Bringing clarity to concept user experience, pp. 1–12 (2011)
29. Ferraz de Abreu, J., Almeida, P., Beça, P.: InApp questions – an approach for contextual evaluation of applications. In: Abásolo, M.J., Almeida, P., Pina Amargós, J. (eds.) jAUTI 2016. CCIS, vol. 689, pp. 163–175. Springer, Cham (2017). https://doi.org/10.1007/978-3-319-63321-3_12

Exploring User Feedbacks: The Basis of a Recommender System of Informative Videos for the Elderly

David Campelo[✉] ⓘ, Telmo Silva ⓘ, and Jorge Abreu ⓘ

Digimedia (CIC.DIGITAL), Aveiro University, Campus Universitário Santiago, Aveiro, Portugal
{david.campelo,tsilva,jfa}@ua.pt

Abstract. Given the popularity of television among older people, technologies based on this device represent a valuable alternative to promote info-inclusion of the senior population, enhancing well-being, autonomy and consequent improving their quality of life. However, to provide a better viewing experience, it is vital to use a personalized approach, which privileges the individual by dynamically learning users' preferences and interests. In the scope of +TV4E project an Interactive TV (iTV) platform is being developed to provide these citizens with personalized information about public and social services from which they could benefit. This research aims to assess seniors' preferences by identifying possible explicit and implicit feedbacks, such as up/down voting and amount of video viewed, retrieved from interactions performed within the iTV application. This paper describes the methodology used to define an adequate interaction scheme to learn seniors' preferences based on these feedbacks, in a participatory and iterative design process, with 14 seniors. Such scheme will support the +TV4E content recommender system in selecting and matching the informative contents with the users' interests more accurately.

Keywords: Interactive TV · Personalization · Recommender systems · Seniors
Feedbacks · Preferences

1 Introduction

Increasing human longevity is, by many reasons, an achievement to be celebrated, but it can be very problematic both for the individuals themselves and for those around them if no proper conditions for being independent, active, and healthy for a longer time are made available [1]. To promote greater levels of participation and autonomy in old age, a set of technological solutions to support seniors' daily activities in a more reliable and secure manner have been developed, in areas ranging from health, mobility and leisure to communication and work [2]. In this context, given the popularity of television among seniors in a daily basis [3–6], some of these technological solutions have used this device to improve wellbeing and quality of life by adding interactive features to the traditional television experience [7].

© Springer International Publishing AG, part of Springer Nature 2018
M. J. Abásolo et al. (Eds.): jAUTI 2017, CCIS 813, pp. 75–89, 2018.
https://doi.org/10.1007/978-3-319-90170-1_6

Particularly in Portugal, seniors often face recurrent scenarios of info-exclusion [8], low literacy levels [9] and digital divide [10], which makes them unaware of information regarding public and social services from which they could benefit (e.g. health campaigns, income taxes notifications, and laws changing alerts). Thus, in order to follow the European Commission orientations for sustainable development and active ageing [11], Portuguese public authorities have been investing strongly in new communication channels to disseminate information about public and social services [12]. These channels have been playing a vital role for Portuguese citizens to obtain valuable information on various governmental assignments. In this context, the +TV4E project comes up with a platform to which proposes an iTV platform to deliver informative videos about public and social services tailored for Portuguese seniors [13].

The +TV4E platform aims to take advantage of the proximity and familiarity seniors have with the television to enable an enriched viewing experience, featuring the integration of informative videos automatically generated from a set of predefined news and institutional Web feeds [14, 15]. Then, these generated videos are pushed to the end-users through an iTV application, which in turn, is in charge of interleaving them with the linear TV broadcasted presentation, according to short interruptions [13]. To achieve a more personalized approach, this study aims to assess the preferences of seniors as end-users of +TV4E platform. To this end, the present research sets out to identify and classify implicit and explicit data, retrieved from interactions performed within the iTV application, which may somehow infer users' interests. Such interactions are on the basis of an interaction scheme, which will support the construction of the user preferences on the informative videos. Therefore, this study plays a major role in the conceptual phase of the recommender system.

The remainder of this paper is structured as follows: The next section presents some related works on recommender systems of TV and video as well as user feedbacks and user profile construction. The third section describes the methodology used to define the interaction scheme, including a literature review, exploratory interviews with users which took part in the preliminary tests of the +TV4E platform, and finally tests with high-fidelity prototypes conducted with seniors recruited from an adult day care centre. The forth section is dedicated to discussions and practical challenges, while the fifth and last section highlights the main conclusions and future works arising from this study, especially with respect to the context of +TV4E platform.

2 Related Work

2.1 Recommender Systems of TV and Video Contents

The advent of Smart TVs, the expansion of TV program/contents and the popularization of VOD (Video on Demand) platforms have contributed to an exponential growth of video contents available. Most of these contents are accessible through many different screen devices (e.g. smartphones, tablets, TVs) and transmitted using broadband (e.g. Internet) and broadcasted TV (e.g. terrestrial, satellite, and cable) networks [14]. On the one hand, there are obvious advantages and, as such, benefits to viewers in having a wide range of reachable contents. However on the other hand, such a huge amount of video contents has enforced TV/set-top box manufacturers, broadcasters, content producers and streaming providers to search for automatic tools to support users in decisions about what to watch next, and thus, offer a more personalized viewing experience [14]. These tools are composed by algorithms and data collection schemes that predict and recommend contents (or items) matching users' interests and/or needs, in the so-called recommender systems [15]. Therefore, in order to provide an enhanced experience for these viewers during the discovery of new content, several pay-TV services providers and research projects have benefited from recommender systems to cope with this scenario of information overload [16].

With the expansion of digital networks and the increase of the number of channels, TV program recommender systems turned into the most popular application of personalized recommender systems for video contents [17]. These systems "assist TV watchers by recommending interesting TV programmes to watch more comfortably and avoiding the traditional way of channel surfing" [18]. First implementations of TV program recommender systems emerged in the 1990s and aimed at suggesting programs from the Electronic Programming Guide (EPG) [19]. Nowadays, some of the most complex and renowned recommender systems are implemented by online streaming services [16], such as Netflix [19] and Youtube [20].

As reported by Kumar and Sharma [17], there has been a significant increase in the movie recommender systems in the scientific literature, like MovieLens [21], a platform which recommends movies based on user past preferences; and Hulu [22], an VOD service which suggests movies and TV shows streamed to internet-connected devices at any time. Véras and his colleagues [16] conducted a broad literature review to analyse and classify scientific works according to different aspects of recommender systems in the TV domain, such as the recommended item types, algorithms, architectural models, output devices, user profiling, and evaluation. These authors reviewed techniques, methods, and applications of 282 studies published between 2003 and 2015 and among the main findings, it is worth to mention the growing focus on recommender systems of video contents beyond the traditional TV programs accessible through an EPG. It was noticed an increasing amount of studies using Web (browser) and mobile platforms as output devices for TV and TV-related contents, creating relevant opportunities for research on new types of video contents in multiple sources of information (e.g. cross-domain recommendation).

The main task of a recommender system for video services is to provide viewers with content suggestions they will most probably be interested in watching. To achieve this, these systems essentially estimate how much a user will like a given content, predicting how relevant it will be for the viewer using one or more prediction (or filtering) techniques [15]. Common examples of prediction techniques are collaborative filtering and content-based filtering. In the classical collaborative filtering technique, suggestions for a specific user are calculated based on the similarity between their interactions in the system, since individuals of similar interactions should have similar tastes [15]. Thus, in this technique users are clustered according to their behaviours in the past to predict potentially interesting items using similarity between clusters. On the other hand, content-based filtering prediction technique is based on descriptive data of recommended items to find items similar to those ones consumed previously, since past interests and tendencies are indicators of future preferences [15].

Barneveld and Setten [23] presented a generic prediction model for a TV recommender system (see Fig. 1). In this model, the prediction technique process calculates a probable interest value of a TV program for a given user, which consists in the item prediction (or suggestion). This process has as input all knowledge stored in the user profile, on items' data and metadata information, and on profiles of other users. Prediction techniques learn the interests and preferences of users from their feedbacks, which are basically constituted by direct and indirect interactions with the system. Some techniques may also provide users with explanations about their reasoning for providing a given item suggestion (e.g. "Because you enjoyed that one, you may like that also"). Optionally, a set of internal validity indicators may be employed to improve predictions when multiple prediction techniques are combined [23].

Fig. 1. Generic prediction model [23].

In order to create an intuitive, easy-to-use iTV application, tailored for seniors, to present informative videos along with regular TV broadcasted contents, this study particularly focuses on the possible feedbacks and interactions viewers would perform to support +TV4E recommender system in learning their preferences and interests with respect to these videos.

2.2 User Profile and Feedbacks in Recommender Systems of TV and Video Contents

According to Iglesias and his colleagues [24], the user profile concept can be defined as "a description of the user interests, characteristics, behaviours, and preferences". In general, user profiles can be constructed in a lot of different ways [14]. Many of the very earliest systems used to ask users to build their own profiles by actively providing information in the terms of items or characteristics they would be interested in. However, sometimes this turns out to be rather confusing and time-consuming for users. Hence, for more compelling and acceptable process of eliciting preferences, a user profile should also consider regular user actions and parameters (e.g. watching time, subscriptions, keywords used in search). Moreover, apart from the prediction technique or algorithm chosen to generate personalized item suggestions, data concerning relationships between users and these items must be collected by the recommender system. These interactions support the recommender system in learning the interest of a given user regarding the items that were somehow consumed.

In the particular case of TV and video services, there are two ways to obtain user interaction data to compose a user profile [14]: by analysing their behaviour during the viewing experience, which is called *implicit feedback*; and by requesting *explicit feedbacks*, which is when the user provides their opinions on a given content. So, user profiles can be built upon direct requests to users, which are clearly defining their positions in relation to the video contents; or by monitoring the system usage and user behaviour, based on interactions that may be indirectly linked to viewers' interests [14].

The main difference between implicit and explicit feedbacks is the main purpose of the associated interaction. In the implicit feedback, user is just following the normal system flow and performing interactions whose main purposes are not to inform a preference or an interest. Implicit feedback interactions range from global actions, such as the amount of time spent watching a video, to detailed actions (e.g. buttons pressed on remote control) [20, 23]. Though at the first place, these actions were envisioned by the system developers to perform a functional task, they may also infer how interested the user is in a content. In explicit feedback, in contrast, users evaluate the relevance and utility of a video, which is generally done by rating it.

According to [25], the simplest and most straightforward approach to elicit users' interest on a certain item is by actively asking them. However, explicit requests for feedback may also be annoying to and inefficient, since user's perceptions regarding the options presented may be quite subjective and divergent. For example, what does it really mean to give 4 out of 5 in star rating? More demanding users might have a very different judgment from less demanding users. In addition, users may be not interested in giving their opinions as it usually breaks their normal experience [25]. In addition, as providing explicit feedbacks usually distracts users from the TV and video viewing experience, requesting them should be as discreet and simple as possible [23, 25].

User feedbacks collected by recommender systems are intrinsically related to contents (or items) and the graphic interface. Some of the most common interfaces used for requesting explicit feedbacks are [25]: (i) scale ratings, where the user evaluates an item based on a scale, from the least to the most interesting/relevant; and (ii) up-down voting, where only two values are used to indicate the user's opinion.

As using explicit ratings is not enough to generate reliable recommendations [26], considering implicit interaction data is crucial to generate recommendations more accurately. However, for many applications it may be very challenging to relate or even quantify these interactions with respect to user preferences, specially to infer negative preferences. For example, considering the example of recommending online texts, what would it mean to spend only half of the average reading time on an electronic article? Several additional components would have to be analysed (e.g. average user read time, subject and word quantity of the article). Additionally, it is worth noticing that often the collection of implicit data is done asynchronously. Thus, in case of momentary network breakdowns, the precision of the implicit feedback may be affected.

Netflix is one of the most popular TV and video streaming services, with almost 100 million subscribers worldwide. In this service, both explicit and implicit feedbacks are used to compose user profiles [19]. Implicit feedbacks include information about partially or completely viewed content and content searching; while explicit feedbacks mainly include user voting data, which used to be implemented in a 5-star rating approach (see Fig. 2). Recently, however, this approach has changed to a thumbs up-down voting system in order to avoid subjectivities of scale ratings as well as to create a simpler approach to viewers [28].

Fig. 2. Netflix Daredevil details screen [28].

Considering that user interaction data is just a fraction of the viewing experience, Youtube recommender system [20] also uses both data retrieved implicitly and explicitly from users as input for its recommender system. Explicit data include favoriting, sharing or liking (thumbs up-down voting) a video, and subscribing to a channel; while implicit data is extracted from users' watching time and interacting with videos history (e.g. viewer started to watch a video, viewer watched a large portion of the video, viewer saved a video to a playlist).

3   Methods

The present study aims to enhance the +TV4E platform by providing an individual approach to the suggested informative videos. Particularly, the present study was part of the conceptual phase of the +TV4E recommender system development [28] and aimed to find adequate answers for the following research questions:

[RQ1] What implicit and explicit data gathered from interactions performed within the +TV4E iTV application could represent seniors' preferences on informative videos?

[RQ2] What associated weights each of these interactions should have to provide more accurate content suggestions to seniors?

The process of identifying and weighting interactive actions seniors may perform within +TV4E iTV application was a spiral and evolutionary process, where the outputs of a given phase served as input for the subsequent step to evolve, improve and validate the interaction scheme proposed by this study.

The initial part of this research consisted in an exploratory approach, a literature review to gather information about commonly used implicit and explicit feedbacks in TV and video services. Table 1 lists feedbacks used by recommender systems of TV and video contents. It is worth noting that, though many scientific studies clearly define the interactions used as input for their respective recommender system, no metrics or weights are associated to any of them.

Table 1. Feedbacks commonly used by recommender systems of TV and video.

Implicit	Explicit
Amount of watching time [16, 20, 21, 23, 24]	5-star rating scale [16, 20, 22]
Favorited contents [16, 21]	Up-down voting [16, 21]
Subscribed content channel [21]	Questionnaires [22]
Search history [20, 23]	Content tagging [22]
Remote control general key logging [24]	

Considering the interactions listed on Table 1, a draft interaction scheme was designed. To enable a less annoying experience for seniors as consumers of +TV4E informative videos, this scheme counted with two feedback approaches only: an up-down voting request to explicitly get seniors' opinions presented by the end of the video exhibition only and the implicitly collected amount of watched time. Thus, data would be collected according to five possible interaction scenarios and their respective weights (Fig. 3): Video not started (weight 0); Exhibition interrupted before 50% of video time (weight −1); Exhibition interrupted between 50% and 100% of video time (weight +1); Exhibition completed and user voted up (like) (weight +2); and Exhibition completed and user voted down (dislike) (weight −2). In this scheme integer values would be used to weight the interaction scenarios (see Fig. 3), which is a simpler and easily implemented solution.

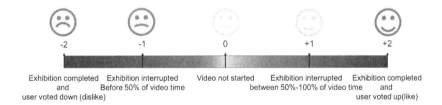

Fig. 3. First interaction scheme.

An evolution of this scheme would consist of a more elaborate and complex approach to calculate the implicit score associated to the viewing experience. Instead of using integer values in a small set of possible scenarios only, and moving from a negative value to a positive value abruptly at 50% of video watched, it would be assigned a proportional weight per percentage of the video watched (see Fig. 4).

Figure 4 shows how this interaction scheme works, with fractional weight values ranging from −1 to 1. If the user interrupts the video exhibition before a given time, a negative value will be assigned to that viewing experience, otherwise a positive value would be assigned. Additionally, in the same way as the first scheme an up-down voting explicit request could be used to collect users' opinions, which would assign maximum and minimum values to the viewing experience: +2 (up) and −2 (down).

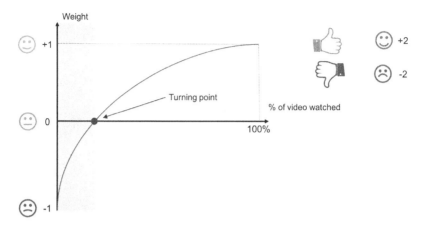

Fig. 4. Second interaction scheme.

In order to assess preferences of seniors, it was set out a participatory and iterative design process. Firstly, a minor set of users which had took part in the preliminary tests of the +TV4E platform were called to an exploratory interview. Afterwards, a larger group of seniors was recruited to provide their opinions on the implicit and explicit feedbacks selected to build up the platform profile.

Phase I – Exploratory interviews with seniors
The first step in the participatory process with seniors consisted of validating the interaction schemes with a random set of users which took part in the +TV4E platform preliminary tests. So, before implementing any high-fidelity prototype, three seniors who had used this platform during its preliminary tests were selected to provide their opinions on the explicit and implicit feedbacks used to assess their preferences on video contents.

The approach selected to this phase included a semi-structured interview guide (see questions in Table 2) to be applied at the participants' homes. This approach enabled higher levels of flexibility in the interviewing process and created a more casual environment in the interviews [32]. All interviews were conducted in September 2017, and participants were one male and two females, aged over 59 years. Questions addressed in the interviews are stated in Table 2 and were defined considering the context of +TV4E platform.

Answers from all three interviews were mostly similar. On Question 1, seniors stated that the remote control should have a special button to tell their impressions on the videos. Regarding questions 2 and 3, all of them agreed that interrupting a given video could be used as an indicative of lack of interest, and the amount of watched time would be proportional to the interest. Thus, the more compelling is the video content, the more they would watch it, having the initial part of the video a larger role in determining the video viewing experience, like in the second interaction scheme (see Fig. 4). Question 4, which aimed at assessing the explicit feedbacks, had divergent answers. One interviewee felt more comfortable with the five-star rating approach, since this concept, which also has been used in hotel ratings, would be more familiar. On the other hand,

Table 2. Exploratory questions on explicit and implicit feedbacks.

1	Suppose that a given video content was not of your interest, how do you imagine this preference could be notified to the platform?
2	If you interrupt the video exhibition, should this interaction be considered as an indicative of a lack of interest on the respective content?
3	Considering that the initial part of the video may contain an overview of the informative content, should interrupting the video exhibition during this overview be considered as an indicative of even less interest on the respective content?
4	How about the system explicitly request your opinion after the video exhibition? How many options seems to be appropriate? Two options (I like it/I do not like it)? Or a five star rating scale?
5	How often should the system request your opinion?

the other two interviewees said that having two or three different options (e.g. I like it, I do not like, I don't like or dislike it) would be more adequate and easier to use. Finally, on question 5 all interviewees said that explicit requests should be optional, and the system should ask their opinion a few times a day only, otherwise it would be very disturbing.

Findings from these exploratory interviews helped to confirm some assumptions as well as introduced some new perceptions on video consumption with +TV4E platform usage. Except for the requests of special buttons on the remote control to explicitly rate video contents, no new implicit or explicit feedbacks were identified. Finally, considering the conflicting answers given to Question 4 it was decided to implement two different rating screen prototypes to support the next phase of this study.

Phase II – Tests with high-fidelity prototypes of explicit rating screens
The second and final step of this study consisted of implementing and testing high-fidelity prototypes of explicit rating screens with collaboration of a broader set of potential users. This phase aimed to gather more substantial insights on the explicit and implicit feedbacks to be implemented by the +TV4E platform. The prototypes consisted of two different types of explicit inputs: 5-star rating (see Fig. 5a) and up-down voting (see Fig. 5b).

Fig. 5. High-fidelity prototype of rating screens: (a) 5-star rating and (b) up-down voting.

Participants recruited to this phase were selected by convenience among seniors enrolled in an adult day care centre of Aveiro, Portugal. The tests were conducted in September, 2017, and for the sample selection, the inclusion criteria were ageing over 64 years old, watching television regularly and being able to read. The group of interviewees (n = 11) included seven females (63.6%) and four males (36.4%), aged over 69 years. All invited participants demonstrated their willingness to help and collaborate.

Unlike in the first phase of exploratory interviews, data collected in this phase was not gathered at participants' homes, but in a controlled environment set up, at the adult day care centre (Fig. 6). Nevertheless, it was attempted to create a relaxed environment, making clear that it was not intended to assess participants' technical skills, but the utility and relevance of the +TV4E platform itself. In addition, in order to keep participants motivated and tuned to the tests, whenever possible conversations about the participant's daily life was held, such as TV shows they watch and hobbies. According to [29], this is an important strategy to be followed due to a recurring "reluctance of older people in talking about technologies".

Fig. 6. Tests in controlled environment, at the adult day care centre.

As none of the participants had any previous contact with the +TV4E platform, it was adopted a cognitive walkthrough [30] approach to make them comfortable with the platform purposes and usage in a short time. By using this technique, participants were asked to perform a sequence of common TV and video consumption tasks, such as watching linear TV and +TV4E informative videos, changing channels, and so on. After getting minimally used to the platform usage, the same exploratory questions defined for the Phase I (see Table 2) were addressed, and along with the Question 4, both explicit rating screens (see Fig. 5) were presented. Due to time and resource constraints, the rating screens were not fully integrated into the +TV4E platform, but were accessible through a special key on the remote only.

During the tests, it was clear that being supported by a high-fidelity prototype is crucial to provide interviewees with a more solid and tangible idea of the research aims.

In addition, using the same semi-structured interview guide in both participatory design phases ensured that the same kind of information would be collected, and thus, helped to build more comparable results.

Like in Phase I, answers were mostly similar. On Questions 1 and 2, all participants said they would interrupt the video exhibition somehow if the content was not interesting at any time (e.g. turn off the TV, change channel, stop video exhibition). On Question 3, all participants said that the amount of video watched could be considered as an indicative of interest, with the initial part having a greater weight. There was no unanimity on Question 4 again, the large majority of participants (81.9%) considered that the up-down voting screen was more usable. In addition, the concept of like/dislike hands was easier to understand and, sometimes, considered more joyful by the participants. Regarding Question 5, six participants (54.5%) agreed to give their opinions after every video exhibition, while others (45.5%) said it would be very annoying and recommended to request for their opinions a few times a day only.

Findings from this phase helped to find the most suitable explicit rating screen to elicit seniors' preferences on informative videos. Using a simpler and less obtrusive approach, such as a like/dislike rating screen, should be more adequate, though such screen should be shown occasionally only.

4   Discussion

Identifying proper data driving content suggestions plays an essential role in the development process of any recommender system, and independently from the prediction or filtering technique strategy implemented, the system must learn users' interests by collecting feedbacks in order to provide more personalized recommendations [31].

Recommender systems of TV and video contents often rely on implicit feedbacks to build up user profiles, which deal with incremental updates on user's viewing history. Though implicit feedbacks may be noisier than explicit feedbacks, they are so ubiquitous that using them effectively can lead to more accurate suggestions [20]. This implicit nature of profiling enables a less disturbing experience, but also represents a challenge for system developers, as implicit data is less obvious to identify and to interpret. If a user has watched a video for only a couple of seconds, probably it's a negative sign, but what if the user has watched half the video? To what extent this experience was more positive than the previous one? It seems rather inefficient and arbitrary to require a minimum amount of video to achieve a positive score.

It is essential to consider the context of the +TV4E platform to define an adequate interaction scheme to assess seniors' preferences on informative videos and to build a proper user profile. Videos generated by this platform usually have a news structure style (i.e. the initial part of the video carries a content overview, *aka* lead[1]). The user interest in each content would be proportional to the amount of watched time (i.e. weights grow over time), having the initial part a greater weight in the score attributed

---

[1]   https://en.wikipedia.org/wiki/News_style.

to the viewing experience (see Fig. 4). Thus, as the user watches a given video the initially negative weight gradually turns into a positive value after the lead is presented[2].

Findings from interviews and tests contributed to choose the second interaction scheme (see Fig. 4), being the lead time of the informative video the turning point in the positive-negative scale of viewing experience. The turning point value should range between 10 and 20% of the video. Adopting a continuous heuristic seems to be a less disruptive and more precise alternative than the first interaction scheme (see Fig. 3), which uses integer values only and an arbitrary value of 50% of minimum watching time to assign a positive value to the viewing experience. In addition, using non-integers weight values should be more effective and appropriate, though it clearly has a more complex implementation.

If making correlations between implicit feedbacks and user interests may be a rather labour-intensive and error-prone task, using explicit feedbacks, on the other hand, is a straight-forward strategy and often tells more about the user experience [15]. However, considering the +TV4E platform and its end-users, graphical interfaces should be as simple and less demanding for user inputs as possible, and thus explicit feedback requests would be preferably implemented should as a simple up-down voting, which could be optional for users to answer, and it should be presented with a countdown after the video presentation. In this way, it is expected to diminish the potential impact in the overall TV and informative video viewing experience. Explicit requests could be implemented as an advanced feature also, accessible at any time of the video presentation and available until few seconds after the presentation is finished, with a countdown. In addition, since only a visual notification of new video suggestion could go unnoticed by users (due to occasional hearing limitations of seniors), it would be advisable to use sound notifications in addition to the regular visual notification. Finally, though some seniors requested to use special buttons to tell their impressions on informative videos, assigning these buttons would possibly demand major changes in the platform as all remote-control keys are often reserved for specific system functionalities and designing a new remote would require extra costs.

5   Conclusions and Future Works

Challenges and opportunities of an ageing population, both at a personal and community level, are still drawing attention of public and private institutions [1, 33] due to the recurring info-exclusion [8], low literacy levels [9] and digital divide [10] among senior population. In this sense, technologies play an important role to promote higher levels of quality of life and independency by providing them with information about public and social services. In addition, to effectively provide more adequate and high-valued information, such technologies should be implemented considering personalization techniques.

This study is part of the conceptual phase of the +TV4E recommender system development [28], and in order to provide more accurate and personalized content suggestions, we set out a process to identify and weight feedbacks gathered from seniors

---

[2] An example of video generated by the platform is available at https://youtu.be/smZIA9oUad0.

interactions to elicit their interests on informative videos presented by the +TV4E platform. These implicit and explicit feedbacks composed an interaction scheme that will support the recommender system in optimizing video suggestions. For a more unobtrusive viewing experience, it was chosen to use the amount of watching time as implicit collected data and an up-down voting request as explicit feedback from seniors.

The main goal of any recommender systems is to provide users with contents in which they would be possibly interested. If defining *what* content should be suggested is essential, selecting *when* it would be presented may be indispensable, imperative for providing seniors with a compelling viewing experience, as good or bad timing may determine the openness of the users to receive the information provided. Therefore, further studies on defining the most relevant moment for content delivery are under discussion. Also, contextual aspects influencing content suggestion will also be addressed soon.

Finally, as the conceptual phase is concluded, future works involve the recommender system implementation and integration with the currently implemented +TV4E platform [15]. As expected, this work includes the proper implementation of the rating screens and implicit feedbacks also. Afterwards, the integrated system will be validated in a series of field tests to evaluate the real accuracy of the recommender system.

Acknowledgements. The first author would like to thank the Brazilian National Council for Scientific and Technological Development (CNPq) for providing a research productivity scholarship to support his doctoral thesis development (process 204935/2014-8).

The +TV4E project has received funding from Project 3599 – Promover a Produção Científica e Desenvolvimento Tecnológico e a Constituição de Redes Temáticas (3599-PPCDT) and European Commission Funding FEDER (through FCT: Fundação para a Ciência e Tecnologia I.P. under grant agreement no. PTDC/IVC-COM/3206/2014).

References

1. Walker, A.: Active ageing: realising its potential. Australas. J. Ageing **34**, 2–8 (2015)
2. Fozard, J.L., Rietsema, J., Bouma, H., Graafmans, J.A.M.: Gerontechnology: creating enabling environments for the challenges and opportunities of aging. Educ. Gerontol. **26**, 331–344 (2000). https://doi.org/10.1080/036012700407820
3. Martins, C.: As novas dinâmicas do consumo audiovisual em portugal 2016. ERC – Entidade Reguladora para a Comunicação Social, Lisboa (2016)
4. Ofcom: The Communications Market Report. http://stakeholders.ofcom.org.uk/market-data-research/market-data/communications-market-reports/cmr15/
5. OBERCOM: Perfil dos consumidores de TDT e de Televisão Paga em Portugal. https://obercom.pt/perfil-dos-consumidores-de-tdt-e-de-televisao-paga-em-portugal-documento-suplementar-do-relatorio-a-televisao-digital-terrestre-em-portugal-futuro-e-desafios/
6. Nielsen: The Total Audience Report: Q1 (2016). http://www.nielsen.com/us/en/insights/reports/2016/the-total-audience-report-q1-2016.html
7. Blackburn, S., Brownsell, S., Hawley, M.S.: A systematic review of digital interactive television systems and their applications in the health and social care fields. J. Telemed. Telecare **17**, 168–176 (2011)

8. Amaro, F., Gil, H.: The "Info-(ex/in)-clusion" of the elderly people: remarks for the present and for the future. In: ED-MEDIA 2011–World Conference on Educational Multimedia, Hypermedia & Telecommunications, pp. 1024–1030 (2011)

9. Instituto Nacional de Estatística: Censos 2011: Resultados Definitivos - Portugal. Lisboa, Portugal (2012)

10. Friemel, T.N.: The digital divide has grown old: determinants of a digital divide among seniors. New Media Soc. **18**, 313–331 (2016). https://doi.org/10.1177/1461444814538648

11. European Commission: A Quality Framework for Services of General Interest in Europe. Commission of European Communities COM, 900 final, Brussels (2011)

12. European Commission: eGovernment in Portugal, Ed. 2.0. https://joinup.ec.europa.eu/page/egovernment-factsheets

13. Ricci, F., Rokach, L., Shapira, B. (eds.): Recommender Systems Handbook. Springer, Boston (2015)

14. Chang, N., Irvan, M., Terano, T.: A TV program recommender framework. Procedia Comput. Sci. **22**, 561–570 (2013)

15. Véras, D., Prota, T., Bispo, A., Prudencio, R., Ferraz, C.: A literature review of recommender systems in the television domain. Expert Syst. Appl. **42**, 9046–9076 (2015)

16. Lu, J., Wu, D., Mao, M., Wang, W., Zhang, G.: Recommender system application developments: a survey. Decis. Support Syst. **74**, 12–32 (2015)

17. Kumar, B., Sharma, N.: Approaches, issues and challenges in recommender systems: a systematic review. Indian J. Sci. Technol. **9**, (2016). https://doi.org/10.17485/ijst/2015/v8i1/94892

18. Cotter, P., Smyth, B.: PTV: intelligent personalised TV guides. In: Proceedings of the Seventeenth National Conference on Artificial Intelligence and Twelfth Conference on Innovative Applications of Artificial Intelligence. pp. 957–964. AAAI Press, London (2000)

19. Gomez-Uribe, C., Hunt, N.: The Netflix recommender system: algorithms, business value, and innovation. ACM Trans. Manag. **6**(4), 13 (2016)

20. Davidson, J., Liebald, B., Liu, J., Nandy, P., Van Vleet, T., Gargi, U., Gupta, S., He, Y., Lambert, M., Livingston, B.: The YouTube video recommendation system. In: Proceedings of the Fourth ACM Conference on Recommender Systems, pp. 293–296. ACM (2010)

21. Harper, F., Konstan, J.A.: The movielens datasets: history and context. ACM Trans. Interact. Intell. **5**(4), 16 (2016)

22. Xiang, L.: Hulu's Recommendation System. http://tech.hulu.com/blog/2011/09/19/recommendation-system.html

23. Barneveld, J.Van, Setten, M.Van: Designing usable interfaces for TV recommender systems. Hum.-Comput. Interact. **6**, 259–286 (2004)

24. Iglesias, J.A., Angelov, P., Ledezma, A., Sanchis, A.: Creating evolving user behavior profiles automatically. IEEE Trans. Knowl. Data Eng. **24**, 854–867 (2012)

25. Nuñez-valdez, E.R., Cueva-lovelle, J.M., Sanjuan, O., Montenegro-marin, C.E., Hernandez, G.I.: Social voting techniques: a comparison of the methods used for explicit feedback in recommendation systems. Int. J. Artif. Intell. Interact. Multimed. **1**, 62–67 (2011)

26. Rastogi, P.: Syst. Eval. Soc. Recommendation Syst.: Challenges Future **7**, 158–166 (2016)

27. Statista: Number of Netflix streaming subscribers worldwide from 3rd quarter 2011 to 1st quarter (2017). https://www.statista.com/statistics/250934/quarterly-number-of-netflix-streaming-subscribers-worldwide/. (in millions)

28. Lincoln, K.: Why Netflix Is Smart to Ditch the 5-Star Rating System. http://www.vulture.com/2017/03/netflix-killing-the-five-star-rating-is-a-good-idea.html

29. Kvale, S.: Interviews: An Introduction to Qualitative Research Interviewing. Sage Publications, Thousand Oaks (1996)

30. Silva, T., Abreu, J.F., Pacheco, O., Almeida, P.: User identification: a key factor for elderly viewers to benefit from interactive television services. In: Cruz-Cunha, M.M., Varajão, J., Powell, P., Martinho, R. (eds.) ENTERprise Information Systems, pp. 40–48. Springer, Heidelberg (2011). https://doi.org/10.1007/978-3-642-24352-3_5
31. Wharton, C., Rieman, J., Lewis, C., Polson, P.: The cognitive walkthrough method: a practitioner's guide. In: Nielson, J., Mack, R. (eds.) Usability Inspection Methods, pp. 105–140. Wiley, New York (1994)
32. Portugal, I., Alencar, P., Cowan, D.: Requirements Engineering for General Recommender Systems. arXiv Prepr. arXiv1511.05262 (2015)
33. Harper, S.: Economic and social implications of aging societies. Science (80-.) **346**, 587–591 (2014)

Omnidirectional Video and Video Repositories

Multi-device Content Based on Video. A Practical Toolset for Creation and Delivery

Joan Llobera[1]([✉]) [iD], Isaac Fraile[1] [iD], Juan A. Núñez[1] [iD], Szymon Malewski[2] [iD], Xavier Artigas[1] [iD], and Sergi Fernandez[1] [iD]

[1] i2cat Foundation, C/Gran Capità 2-4, 08035 Barcelona, Spain
joan.llobera@i2cat.net
[2] PSNC, Jana Pawła II 10, 61-139 Poznań, Poland

Abstract. The arrival of head mounted displays (HMDs) to the contemporary living room extends the need for producing content that works for the television and companion screen devices. In this work we introduce a set of three tools that can be used for the production and delivery of synchronous multi-device content, across the TV, companion screens and HMDs. The production tool is implemented as a custom Adobe Premiere Pro plugin. The publication and delivery process is implemented as an online service controlled through a web application. The content playout is implemented with a multi-device video player that combines video decoding and playout. In this article we introduce the design choices guiding our software development and the different tools we developed to realize it. We also detail some basic measures of system performance on different devices, and propose further steps towards the easy production and delivery of multi-device content.

Keywords: Multi-device synchronization · Multi-device content · Virtual reality
Omnidirectional video

1 Introduction

The majority of TV consumers now watch TV programs in a multi-display environment [9]. Companion screens - most often smartphones - are generally used to check information not directly related to the events in the TV content being watched, or to interact in social media on topics related to the broadcast [4], sometimes at the expense of local social interaction [5]. Broadcasters have tried to orchestrate these different platforms, and there is reason to believe this contributes to user engagement [11]. Traditionally, companion screen applications have been developed ad hoc, and only very recently the industry has considered the need for specific production tools and production processes adapted to the reality of multi-device consumption [8]. In this context, it remains challenging to create and deliver synchronized video across the TV and companion screens, particularly when the goal is to match user expectations and preferences [1].

The arrival of virtual reality devices to the living room introduces more possibilities, but also further challenges. Since traditional video was not conceived to support

© Springer International Publishing AG, part of Springer Nature 2018
M. J. Abásolo et al. (Eds.): jAUTI 2017, CCIS 813, pp. 93–104, 2018.
https://doi.org/10.1007/978-3-319-90170-1_7

Fig. 1. Traditional and omnidirectional video formats. Top: an image typical of a traditional TV showing a football match. An insert informs the consumer that content is also available for tablets and HMDs. Bottom: a capture of an omnidirectional video with inserts of traditional cameras. This content is delivered synchronized with the main TV stream. Image courtesy of Lightbox (www.lightbox.pt).

interactive rendering techniques, the solution generally adopted in the audiovisual industry is the delivery of an omnidirectional video stream. Omnidirectional video is quite different from traditional video: the rendering process requires the image to be projected, typically, on a sphere or on a cube, and only a small portion of the image is rendered, depending on the head orientation of the user, as detected by the HMD (see Fig. 1). As a consequence, an image of much higher quality has to be transmitted to render the same effective quality on the end-user screen.

In this article we introduce our efforts to enable the easy creation and delivery a new form of broadcast multi-device video within the European H2020 ICT project ImmersiaTV [19]. The main challenge addressed is to streamline the creation and delivery of a video-based synchronous experience across displays, including TV, companion screens such as tablets and smartphones, and HMDs. An additional challenge addressed is that we want the content delivered to be device-specific both in terms of video format (omnidirectional or traditional) and on how it supports interactive input (or lacks interaction support, for the case of the TV). For TV, this means that content can be consumed simply by sitting on the couch and watching, without further input, and that the audiovisual language used follows established conventions. For tablets and smartphones, it means that user input works seamlessly with the specificities of each device (head movements for HMDs, or finger-based input for smartphones or tablets).

To address these requirements, we have designed and implemented an end-to-end production, delivery and rendering pipeline for offline content production which specifically addresses these needs. In the following sections we further outline the design principles adopted (Sect. 2), the modules developed and the performance of the critical ones (Sect. 3), and summarize our conclusions, and the next steps we want to pursue (Sect. 4).

2 Design Principles and Related Work

2.1 Synchronous Multi-platform Playout

Typically, people watch TV in their living room. Often, they do so while doing other activities. These can range from engaging in conversation, playing with kids, social interaction on mobile phones, but can also span a myriad different activities. It is therefore unlikely that end-users will be actively engaged in trying different devices for media consumption, and checking what is possible at every time. On the contrary, it seems more likely that they will switch their attention to a particular content or device alternatively with other activities. We must therefore create content that provides experiences which allow for such limited attention span, and which allow the end-user to switch freely between devices.

In addition, if we want end-users to switch to particular devices in particular moments of the experience, we must indicate so across media. This is easy to do by adding overlays within the videos being delivered. For example, at a certain moment in the TV content, a small icon appears to indicate there is additional content available on HMDs. However, to enable such novel applications we must guarantee certain coherence across the overall experience, which seems only possible if we can deliver synchronous playout across devices.

In other terms: to create content for all devices, we need to create content that is adapted to each of them, and play it synchronously [9, 11, 18]. To play synchronized content, we have adapted emerging standards [20] and Gstreamer's version of the Precision Time Protocol (IEEE 1588) [21], as done, for example, in [17]. We have also embraced the use of omnidirectional video for HMDs and smartphones, in order to allow the user to visualize the scene in different directions. To further facilitate user adoption, we have also extended synchronized playout to a web-based player. This allows delivering synchronized experiences also with web browsers.

Through the different devices the audience is still able to watch TV sitting on their couch, or tweet comments about it. However, the audience can also use immersive displays to feel like being inside the audiovisual stream, or use tablets and smartphones to explore these omnidirectional videos, or even, in the future, to zoom in, or share portions of it through social media.

2.2 Portals

In the context of streaming omnidirectional video, we introduce the idea of portals as video inserts that can be rendered in the HMD. The idea of portals is inspired from the homonymous and famous videogame Portal [22]. In the context of video streaming, these portals can be portions of other omnidirectional videos, which allows introducing basic interactive storytelling techniques such as scene selection or forking paths. Portals can also be inserts of traditional or directive videos. Traditional video inserts also allow reintroducing classical audiovisual language that is not possible to render solely with omnidirectional videos, such as close-ups, slow motion, shot-countershot, etc. (see also Fig. 2).

These strategies will not avoid the necessary precautions needed for shooting omnidirectional video [12]. Omnidirectional video requires thinking very carefully about how the end-user's attention is guided within the scene, and has a relatively narrow range of distances where the action is actually perceived clearly. If the action is too close, it will feel very flat, or deformed, and it can rapidly feel appalling for the end-user. If the action is too far, it will be difficult to see by the content consumer. Since omnidirectional video does not allow typical video techniques such as zooming in, or shooting close-ups, we believe it is likely that video inserts can facilitate the portraying of relevant details within the omnidirectional scene.

Actually, video inserts allow reintroducing the entire set of conventions of classic audiovisual language. In addition to close-ups, we believe that classical shooting strategies such as shot-countershots can be adapted to deliver a richer experience in omnidirectional video and help the user transition from traditional media to such emerging formats.

Portals also open the door for richer interaction, either inside the HMD or, since a portal can render the content available on another device, interact between devices. For example, it would be possible to present a video insert that is actually a transition towards another omnidirectional video scene. This enables the easy integration of branching narratives within audiovisual scenes based on omnidirectional video.

Last but not least, an additional reason to consider video inserts as portals is that such metaphor can also work for more immersive media. To understand why this is relevant we must step back, and consider the fact that virtual reality experiences work better when they support sensorimotor correlations [14]. For the case of rendering visual stimuli, this means that when the end-user changes his head position or orientation, the rendered content updates the rendered perspective accordingly. Despite omnidirectional

Fig. 2. The recording setup. Top: a camera setup to record traditional and omnidirectional video simultaneously. Bottom: a schematic diagram of possible directive inserts located within the omnidirectional video. Image courtesy of Lightbox (www.lightbox.pt).

video supports head rotations, it still falls very short at delivering sensorimotor correlations.

In this context, we must consider emerging formats such as free viewpoint video (FVV). Despite free viewpoint video was introduced several years ago [2, 15, 16], and improvements on the ease of production and delivery of such content appear regularly [3, 7], to the best of our knowledge currently there is no easy and cheap commercial solution that enables the intuitive creation of FVV. However, since such formats would radically improve the quality of the virtual reality experience, it is not impossible that the rise of virtual reality displays also comes together with a novel generation of FVV production techniques. In this perspective, the introduction of portals as a means to reintroduce classical audiovisual conventions or branching narratives is particularly promising, due to the fact that portals allow preserving at all times the capability of the content to adapt the perspective to the end-users actions. This is true *even for the content rendered in the portal*. In this way, were FVV made available for production, we could introduce conventions of classical audiovisual language, as well as branching narratives, while preserving place illusion, i.e., the feeling of *being there*. This might seem far-fetched, but given the current pace of media evolution in relation to VR, and the benefits FVV can bring to it, in relation to supporting sensorimotor correlations, it is not completely impossible that such format will have wider industrial adoption.

All in all, from our current perspective, which is focused on trying to identify good design principles to build meaningful multi-device experiences, these different arguments suggest that the consideration of video inserts as portals to be rendered within an omnidirectional scene is a good design choice.

3   An End-to-End Pipeline

Designing and implementing a broadcast audiovisual production chain is challenging due to the diversity of processes, technologies and production practices that it requires. In this section we outline the main solutions, either adopted or implemented, for our purpose, with content examples.

3.1   Capture

The creation of content that is both omnidirectional and traditional requires shooting simultaneously in both content formats. Preliminary tests with separate shootings for omnidirectional and traditional cameras revealed it was unfeasible to synchronize two different shootings, even when the actors in the scene were repeating the same actions.

The solution found by the production team was to use two *BlackMagic Micro Studio Camera 4k* micro-cameras for the traditional shooting, which could be hidden or, if visible, removed in post-production with a reasonably small amount of effort. This combined with an omnidirectional capture rig, which was either composed of 6 GoPro 3 Black Rig cameras, or 3 of them with fish-eye lenses (see Fig. 2) allowed capturing simultaneously traditional and omnidirectional footage. However, for a joint shooting, we must address the fact that omnidirectional cameras capture the whole visual field, and therefore would show the traditional camera and the film crew behind it. This is not problematic for sports or music events, but it goes strongly against the conventions of fiction or documentary.

3.2 Edition

Dedicated stitching tools such as Video-stitch studio by Video-stitch [23], or Autopano by Kolor, allow stitching video footage captured with camera rigs in order to create omnidirectional video. Tools for omnidirectional video edition, such as CaraVR [24] and Mettle's suite [25] allow further post-production. However, we are not aware of an editing tool targeting synchronous rendering across devices. To address this fact, we have designed and implemented a plugin for Adobe's Premiere Pro. The ImmersiaTV Premiere Pro plugin (Fig. 3) allows defining the inserts that are placed within an omni-directional scene, and how they should behave relative to the movements of the user. For example, they can either be static on the screen, or static on the omnidirectional scene. They can also trigger transitions between different omnidirectional videos.

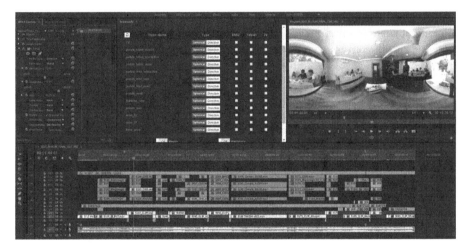

Fig. 3. Video editing tool for multi-platform content. The Adobe Premiere ImmersiaTV panel, shown at the center, allows defining omnidirectional and directive (i.e., traditional) tracks, as well as which devices does each track target. The inserts added to the omnidirectional view, shown at right, can be edited with the ImmersiaTV Portal Effect, whose widgets are shown at the left. Image courtesy of Lightbox (www.lightbox.pt).

The ImmersiaTV Premiere Pro plugin also allows selecting which tracks should be rendered in each of 3 possible devices (TV, tablet or HMD). It works both with Mac and Windows, and has been tested with a variety of video editors.

Since this is the main element allowing creative minds to make design choices in the experience created by multi-device content, we have invested a considerable amount of effort to make sure we integrated with existing features of video edition software, and in particular with Premiere Pro. An example of such features is the use of interactive transitions which are triggered to introduce or conclude a particular video insert. These transitions mimic exactly the behavior and user interface of traditional Premiere Pro transitions, but they are only triggered by the end-users input. Another example is the possibility of using nested sequences to combine different edits, something which has shown extremely useful to combine different tracks in a coherent edit, and then use it in different ways in different devices.

3.3 Encoding

The media encoding uses readily available tools for encoding in H.264 and AAC encoding formats. Adaptive bitrate streaming is based on MPEG-DASH (ISO/IEC 23009-1:2014). Encoding is implemented as a cloud service, running on a Linux server using the Dockers virtualization tool as well as MP4Box from Gpac's MP4Box for MPEG-DASH multiresolution encoding [26]. Video decoding uses the Gstreamer library [27]. The additional metadata required for playout, which relates audiovisual streams with devices (i.e., allows selecting different streams for TVs and tablets), as well as to define interaction and media orchestration requirements, follows closely the format of MPEG-DASH manifests, and its XML specification is publicly available [28]. Content publication is performed through a custom built website (Fig. 4) which allows triggering media conversion, as well as monitoring progress on media encoding and publishing content generating a list of content parsed at the delivery stage.

Fig. 4. The web app allowing to control to trigger the transcoding of the different assets, as well as their publication for consumption.

3.4 Delivery

To combine universality, ease of use and flexibility, we combine an app-based solution together with a player based on web technologies. In both cases, metadata parsing is done with a custom parser, which also generates the appropriate geometry and provides the DASH player with the appropriate DASH manifests.

The web player is based on WebGL and MPEG-DASH, implemented in a module for the generation and reproduction of the contents, and based on three.js and dash.js standard libraries. A second module synchronizes the contents following the DVB-CSS standard. Our web-based solution allows scene rendering without third party players or native applications. It can be served from a Content Delivery Network (CDN), allowing automatic updates of both the contents and the player. In addition, since it is based on web standards, it can be easily adapted to HbbTV solutions. In practice, this solution can reproduce up to 4096 × 2048, with 15 Mbps of bitrate and 30 frames per second. However, web-based solutions are intrinsically limited by the web browser stack to support communication and streaming technologies. For our use case, this has limiting implications for performance, codec constraints and hardware integration.

As an alternative, to facilitate the integration of video rendering with user input on native apps, the simplest option seemed to combine GStreamer, the reference library for multimedia pipelines, and Unity3D, the most accessible game engine for videogame and virtual reality developers. We designed and implemented the GStreamer Unity Bridge (GUB) to realize precisely this. The GUB has three parts. The GStreamer part receives the video and decodes it. This process is based on the GStreamer component playbin, and allows playing at least .mov, mp4 and MPEG-DASH. The texture passing is a key technical element: each frame decoded in GStreamer is passed to Unity3D as a hardware texture, and is suitable for rendering in the standard game engine environment. Specific code for windows (Direct3D 9) and Android (OpenGL-ES 2.0) has been developed for texture passing.

In addition, since copying full textures between system memory and the graphics processing unit (GPU) can have prohibitive performance costs at certain resolutions, particularly in low-end devices such as Android mobile phones, in the Android pipeline we have implemented a *Rendering to Texture* solution based on a Frame Buffer Object. This allows rendering a frame decoded in Gstreamer without leaving the GPU, which brings significant boost in performance. Despite the overhead of handling a 3D Engine like Unity3D, the GUB can play resolutions that are competitive with commercial players (see Table 1). However, we also need to consider that rendering for mobile-based HMD, either cardboard or Samsung GearVR, imposes a double rendering process (one for each eye), which further decreases performance. Therefore, despite we can currently reproduce synchronously video up to 4096 × 2048, bitrate of 50 Megabits per second (Mbps) and 30 frames per second on a Samsung Galaxy S6, this resolution drops to 1024 × 512, bitrate of 2.3 Mbps and 25 frames per seconds when VR rendering is required.

To facilitate user adoption, we have made it publicly available under a LGPL license [29], raising considerable interest (In the first 10 months since it was published, we have had an average of over 250 downloads per month).

Table 1. Performance measurements for different test vectors. We show Frames per Second and a subjective estimate of a Mean Opinion Score by one user. Test vectors are: Hd (1980 × 1080), Bitrate: 3 Mb/s, Framerate: 25, Codec: H264, 2K (2560 × 1440), Bitrate: 3,5 Mb/s, Framerate: 25, Codec: H264; 4K (3840 × 2160), Bitrate: 5 Mb/s, Framerate: 25, Codec: H264 PC is Processor: Intel Core i7-6500U CPU @ 2.50 Ghz, Ram: 16 Gb, Graphics card: Intel Graphics 520, SO: Windows 10 Home edition 64 bits

Device	Test vector	FPS	MOS
Samsung S6	4K	25	5
	2K	25	5
	HD	25	5
Samsung S7	4K	20	4
	2K	25	5
	HD	25	5
Galaxy Tab S	4K	–	0
	2K	20	4
	HD	25 fps	5
PC	4K	25	5
	2K	25	5
	HD	25	5

4   Conclusions and Future Work

We have introduced two simple design principles which, when combined, seem appropriate to address the challenge of creating experiences that integrate TVs, companion screens and HMDs in a coherent experience.

To demonstrate the feasibility of this approach we have developed an end-to-end solution to enable the production and delivery of video-based multi-device synchronous and, at some extent, interactive experiences, with a performance that is comparatively equivalent to standard commercial video players. Performance tests show that the limit in delivered quality is determined by hardware processing load, rather than bandwidth limitations. Further work will be needed to optimize the media quality delivered, particularly for VR-based content, which requires separate renderings for each eye. For this purpose, tiling strategies [10, 13] seem a good direction to explore. For mobile devices, we are also considering a more heterodox DASH client which considers additional factors, beyond bandwidth, to select the most appropriate encoded quality [6].

On the content creation side, further development of content examples exploring more exhaustively the interaction possibilities enabled by inter-device synchronization is a different but complementary work that we would also like to pursue. In this direction, further work to refine and expand the possibilities given by the Premiere Pro plugin here introduced is desirable, particularly regarding the definition of interactive functionality, such as how the consumer's input affects the media being rendered and the overall experience. Its usage with video editors, has showed that, although intuitive, these tools present many limitations, particularly for interactive content. Adopting the fixed time-line characteristic of video, and central to the interaction metaphors on which video-editing software is based, rapidly feels quite limiting when we want to explore richer interactivity. It is therefore possible that, in order to expand the interactive possibilities we must stop using the fixed timeline metaphor, and switch to a node-based software, as typically found in sophisticated post-production solutions.

Globally, the integration of HMDs within the living room consumption habits is still a matter open to speculation. In this context, the evolution of innovative video formats such as FVV, together with the increasing ease with which we can produce mesh-based three dimensional content, as typically found in videogames, raises questions on content format which are difficult to answer beyond trying different options, and studying what works best. In this work we have demonstrated an end-to-end toolset based on simple design choices, and showed it can work in practice.

All in all, we believe the two simple design principles - synchronous playout and portals, and particularly their combination, provide a good starting point from which to design, produce and deliver multi-device experiences. However, the question of whether these principles should be implemented on a video-based pipeline, or an entirely different media format, is one which is still difficult to answer, given the speed of evolution and the variety of formats that are currently being used for VR production.

Acknowledgements. This work has been developed with the support of the European Union's Horizon 2020 programme under grant agreement No. 688619 (www.immersiatv.eu). Developing an end-to-end pipeline requires competent and motivated programmers. In the work here introduced we acknowledge the contributions of Wojciech Kapsa and Daniel Piesik, from PSNC, as well as Ibai Jurado, David Gómez, Einar Meyerson, David Cassany and Juan Gordo from i2cat Foundation.

References

1. Boronat, F., Montagud, M., Marfil, D., Luzón, C.: Hybrid broadcast/broadband TV services and media synchronization: demands, preferences and expectations of spanish consumers. IEEE Trans. Broadcast. (2017)
2. Carranza, J., Theobalt, C., Magnor, M.A., Seidel, H.-P.: Free-viewpoint video of human actors. In: ACM Transactions on Graphics (TOG), pp. 569–577 (2003)
3. Collet, A., Chuang, M., Sweeney, P., Gillett, D., Evseev, D., Calabrese, D., Hoppe, H., Kirk, A., Sullivan, S.: High-quality streamable free-viewpoint video. ACM Trans. Graph. (TOG) **34**(4), 69 (2015)
4. Courtois, C., D'heer, E.: Second screen applications and tablet users: constellation, awareness, experience, and interest. In: Proceedings of the 10th European Conference on Interactive TV and Video, pp. 153–156 (2012)
5. D'heer, E., Courtois, C.: The changing dynamics of television consumption in the multimedia living room. Convergence **22**(1), 3–17 (2016)
6. Gómez, D., Boronat, F., Montagud, M., Luzón, C.: End-to-end DASH platform including a network-based and client-based adaptive quality switching module. In: Proceedings of the 7th International Conference on Multimedia Systems, p. 38 (2016)

7. Huang, J., Chen, Z., Ceylan, D., Jin, H.: 6-DOF VR videos with a single 360-camera. In: Virtual Reality (VR), 2017 IEEE, pp. 37–44 (2017)
8. Meixner, B., Glancy, M., Rogers, M., Ward, C., Röggla, T., Cesar, P.: Multi-screen director: a new role in the TV production workflow? In: Adjunct Publication of the 2017 ACM International Conference on Interactive Experiences for TV and Online Video, pp. 57–62 (2017)
9. Montagud, M., Boronat, F., Stokking, H., van Brandenburg, R.: Inter-destination multimedia synchronization: schemes, use cases and standardization. Multimed. Syst. **18**(6), 459–482 (2012)
10. Niamut, O.A., Thomas, E., D'Acunto, L., Concolato, C., Denoual, F., Lim, S.Y.: MPEG DASH SRD: spatial relationship description. In: Proceedings of the 7th International Conference on Multimedia Systems, p. 5 (2016)
11. Rainer, B., Timmerer, C.: Self-organized inter-destination multimedia synchronization for adaptive media streaming. In: Proceedings of the 22nd ACM International Conference on Multimedia, pp. 327–336 (2014)
12. Sheikh, A., Brown, A., Watson, Z., Evans, M.: Directing attention in 360-degree video, pp. 43–47 (2016). http://dx.doi.org/10.1049/ibc.2016.0029
13. Skupin, R., Sanchez, Y., Hellge, C., Schierl, T.: Tile based HEVC video for head mounted displays (2016)
14. Slater, M.: Place illusion and plausibility in virtual environments. Philos. Trans. R. Soc. B: Biol. Sci. **364**(1535), 3549 (2009)
15. Starck, J., Hilton, A.: Spherical matching for temporal correspondence of non-rigid surfaces. In: Tenth IEEE International Conference on Computer Vision (ICCV 2005), Volume 1, vol. 2, pp. 1387–1394 (2005). https://doi.org/10.1109/iccv.2005.229
16. Starck, J., Miller, G., Hilton, A.: Video-based character animation. In: Proceedings of the 2005 ACM SIGGRAPH/Eurographics Symposium on Computer Animation - SCA 2005, p. 49 (2005). https://doi.org/10.1145/1073368.1073375
17. Veenhuizen, A., van Brandenburg, R.: Frame accurate media synchronization of heterogeneous media sources in an HBB context. In: Media Synchronization Workshop (2012)
18. Vinayagamoorthy, V., Ramdhany, R., Hammond, M.: Enabling frame-accurate synchronised companion screen experiences. In: Proceedings of the ACM International Conference on Interactive Experiences for TV and Online Video, pp. 83–92 (2016)
19. The ImmersiaTV Project. www.immersiatv.eu. Accessed 08 Jan 2018
20. The DVB-CSS Protocol. http://www.etsi.org/deliver/etsi_ts/103200_103299/10328601/ 01.01.01_60/ts_10328601v010101p.pdf. Accessed 08 Jan 2018
21. Description of the Precision Time Protocol, as implemented in the Gstreamer framework. https://gstreamer.freedesktop.org/data/doc/gstreamer/head/gstreamer-libs/html/ GstPtpClock.html. Accessed 08 Jan 2018
22. The Portal Game. http://store.steampowered.com/app/400/. Accessed 08 Jan 2018
23. VideoStitch Studio. https://www.orah.co/software/videostitch-studio/. Accessed 21 Feb 2018
24. CaraVR. https://www.thefoundry.co.uk/products/cara-vr/. Accessed 21 Feb 2018
25. Mettle. https://www.mettle.com. Accessed 21 Feb 2018
26. Gpac. https://gpac.wp.mines-telecom.fr/mp4box/. Accessed 21 Feb 2018
27. Gstreamer. https://gstreamer.freedesktop.org/
28. ImmersiaTV Server. http://server.immersiatv.eu/public_http/metadata/ImmersiaTV.html. Accessed 21 Feb 2018
29. Gstreamer Movie Texture. https://www.assetstore.unity3d.com/en/#!/content/59897. Accessed 21 Feb 2018

A Process to Design a Video Library for Senior Users of iTV

Telmo Silva⁽⊠⁾ ⓘ, Hilma Caravau ⓘ, Martinho Mota ⓘ,
Liliana Reis ⓘ, and Carlos Hernandez ⓘ

CIC.DIGITAL/Digimedia, Department of Communication and Arts,
University of Aveiro, Aveiro, Portugal
{tsilva,hilmacaravau,m.vaz.mota,lilianaareis,cjhs}@ua.pt

Abstract. The adoption rate of technologies by older adults is dependent on
several factors, such as the identified potential benefits in the users' perspective.
In the scope of +TV4E project, which aims to deliver informative videos
regarding public and social services to older people through an interactive television (iTV) platform, this study defines a process to design the video library
allowing the access to the previous referred videos. Therefore, this article
explores the process carried out to define the best design approach to present the
video library. The research was conducted in three phases: (i) video library
design; (ii) usability evaluation and (iii) definition of the final layout. Each phase
included a specific sample of potential end users and different techniques of data
collection were applied. The achieved results for this study revealed that working
with older people is a difficult task and researchers need to be flexible, willing to
adapt the data collection process to eventual needs that come up during a project's
development.

Keywords: Elderly · iTV · Video library · Design · Usability · UX

1 Introduction

Nowadays almost all developed countries are facing an inversion of the ageing pyramid
with an evident growth of the elderly population. Currently, the older population (people
over 60 years old) reached 962 million in 2017, which represents 13% of the total population and it is expected to raise to 1.4 billion worldwide, by 2030 [1]. This phenomenon
presents new challenges to societies at academic and governmental levels, in terms of
finding the best ways to fulfil the needs and expectations of the elderly.

Being informed is a vital pillar to participate in today's society, which is increasingly
becoming more and more dependent on information. Seniors are at a clear disadvantage
when it comes to accessing information about nowadays topics since it is mostly scat-
tered across various mediums such as the internet, which requires a certain level of digital
literacy. However, the quick evolution and the high volume of technological innovations
related to seniors' needs that have emerged in the last decades show that this is a dynamic
area in terms of providing services that can answer their needs. It is important to build
inclusive digital environments that promote easy access to digital tools so that the elderly

© Springer International Publishing AG, part of Springer Nature 2018
M. J. Abásolo et al. (Eds.): jAUTI 2017, CCIS 813, pp. 105–116, 2018.
https://doi.org/10.1007/978-3-319-90170-1_8

can maintain and improve their quality of life [2]. Although, several times, developed technologies did not consider the needs and expectations of the target population which affect the perceived benefits and, consequently, the level of older people's adoption [3]. To avoid this problem and to transform technology into a real asset for the elderly, it is important that they become involved in the development of a product from its early stages, by sharing their perceptions and expectations.

As a response to the identified needs of Portuguese seniors, the +TV4E project aims to promote the info-inclusion of them, through an iTV platform, by interleaving the normal television broadcast with informative spots related to public and social services. This video spots are delivered accordingly user profile [4]. During the definition of functional and technical requirements of this platform, it was observed that a video library would be an added value allowing the visualization of video spots already saw, as well as to access to videos that were triggered but that were not visualized.

This paper aims to present and analyse the process of defining the best design and development approach regarding this video library.

Additionally to this introduction, the article is organized in the following parts: Sect. 2 presenting a theoretical framework on the questions to fulfil the informative seniors' needs and guidelines to follow when building TV interfaces for the elderly; Sect. 3 which illustrates the methodological steps followed to define video library; Sect. 4, where the obtained results are presented and discussed in detail; and finally, Sect. 5 where it is presented some of the conclusions drawn from this study as well as tracks to future work.

2   Theoretical Framework

Worldwide, societies are facing a serious increase in the number of older people. Although this is a very positive phenomenon, supported in several enhancements in many areas of society, a new set of problems and challenges arise. The report of the United Nations [1] reveals that in 2017, 13% of the global population is 60 years old or above, which corresponds to 962 million people. This segment of population is growing at a rate of about 3% per year. Projections indicate that, in 2030, the population over 60 years old will achieve 1.4 million, 2.1 billion in 2050 and could reach 3.1 million in 2100 [1]. This phenomenon is inevitable, concerning the fertility declines and the increase in life expectancy rises hampered by the expected decrease of global population (of 51 countries) between 2017 and 2050 [1].

Specifically, Portuguese resident population projections confirms this tendency and it is expected that, in 2080, the ageing pyramid approaches an inverted triangle shape [5]. Between 2015 and 2080, the number of people who are 65 years old and over will increase from 2.1 to 2.8 million [5].

The "active ageing" concept, is one of the first contributions with a global impact that recognized ageing population as an important phenomenon. This concept encourages older people to remain active by working longer and retiring later, through engaging in volunteer work after retirement, and by leading healthy and autonomous lives. "Active ageing", created by World Health Organization (WHO), is defined as the process of optimizing opportunities in three pillars: health, participation and security [6]. This will promote the elderly's quality of life, highly influenced by the ability to maintain their autonomy and independence.

One of the living areas that influence older people' quality of life is the access to information. This allows people to stay aware about their surrounding environment and consequently make decisions in a more supported manner [7]. In Portugal, despite information about social and public services being available in several service counters and online platforms, this information is sometimes shrouded in technical terms hard to decipher by most citizens. To make this process even more complex, especially to older people, accessing this type of information involves a pro-active behaviour by the user [8]. According to Silva and colleagues [7], informational needs of the Portuguese elderly encompass: health care and welfare services; social services; financial services: cultural, informal education and entertainment; security services; local authority services and transport services.

Technological products can help seniors to improve their quality of life. In this manner, interactive TV applications have a great potential to support seniors' needs mainly due to the fact that they spend lots of time watching television. In this context, an academic project is under development aiming to develop an iTV platform, specially designed for the elderly and based on simple interactions, that delivers information about social and public services through brief video spots without active search required from the user. The video library is an important platform enhancement that strengths the overall solution for the elderly. This feature allows the users to navigate through a list of all generated videos in the last five days. To the development of this feature the research team was guided by the motto: the development of new innovative products should be conducted, since the beginning of the process, with inputs from potential end users that represent the target population [9].

In the beginning of the +TV4E project an extensive study regarding guidelines to follow when building TV interfaces for the elderly has been conducted. This study was focused on a literature review regarding the specific characteristics of the seniors that come from the ageing process, such as loss of hearing and visual acuity [10]. These characteristics need to be taken into account while developing software for seniors to guarantee high acceptance ratio. However, since there is no sound in the video library, only visual-related recommendations were considered, specifically regarding text, icons and colours. The following guidelines were extracted from the study of Reis and colleagues [10] in order to help the design of the library.

Most notably, loss of vision in seniors causes them to have difficulties in focusing at short distances, distinguishing small details, discriminating chromatic differences and reading moving text. It also reduces their adaptability to lighting, makes them more susceptible to brightness and requires them to have more luminosity when reading, for example. To counter these limitations there are several design recommendations to make visual content more suitable for the elderly. In general, the literature suggests that text in screens should be at least 40 pts, serif fonts should be used, opposed to italic or decorative fonts, text should be aligned to the left, the spacing between lines needs to guarantee fluidity and readability and there should be high contrast between the background and the text. When it comes to icons, they should be the combination of an image and text, never one without the other, be easily distinguishable and avoid the use of abstract concepts or graphical conventions associated with recent digital technologies. Lastly, the colours need to be chosen carefully to consider the limited colour spectrum of televisions and the seniors' needs. Concerning this, the development of the video library available on +TV4E platform will take all these orientations into account as well as inputs gathered from potential end users. So, in the coming section, the methodology used to select the preferred layout for the +TV4E platform is described in detail, going over the objectives of the study, the sample and the whole process.

3   Methodology

The present study was held with the main objective of determining and creating a fully functional video library layout that would fulfil the needs of the Portuguese seniors allowing them to access to videos delivered through the +TV4E project iTV application. The main purpose of this video library is to allow the users to visualize the informative videos provided by the platform in a manner similar to an on-demand video service. In the video library, the users are able to re-watch videos they had already seen and watch videos they rejected/missed, therefore complementing their user experience and giving them some degree of control over the system.

Initially, the methodology defined included a design phase [11] followed by a layout presentation to a group of seniors, and the inclusion of the interface layout in the final prototype to be tested at home by potential end users. However, over time, the research team realized that the achieved results should be corroborated with more tests in a laboratory context, to improve the interface layout. The redefinition of the followed methodological steps underwent some changes over time, which transformed this path into an evolutionary process.

The data collection occurred in three key moments (see Fig. 1), with potential end users and different techniques: (i) one focus group with 4 seniors for the video library design; (ii) one cognitive walkthrough and a survey with 11 seniors to evaluate usability, and (iii) one focus group with 4 seniors to define the final layout for the video library.

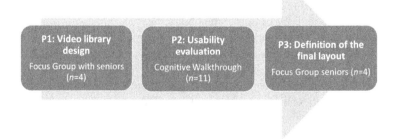

Fig. 1. Phases of the process to define the video library interface

Thereafter, the stages to achieve the final layout of the video library interface and the corresponding process will be described in detail, as well as the sample and process of each phase.

3.1 Video Library Design

Since this work aims to define the best approach for a video library for seniors, before starting off with the first phase of the design process, a state of the art review was conducted to identify trends regarding iTV applications for seniors [11]. Using this state of the art review as a theoretical support, three layout proposals were developed to be validated by the seniors allowing them to choose the most suitable solution. Even though there were three different approaches, all layouts had a similar structure regarding static elements, specifically the header containing the main information and the instruction to return to the TV broadcast. Besides sharing the header, in terms of navigation, all layouts were based on a list of videos generated in the last seven days and sorted chronologically from newest to oldest.

The first layout (Layout 1 - Fig. 2) shows two horizontal navigation lists, where the first one displays the unseen videos while the second list aggregates the seen videos. It is also the simplest proposal since each video card contains only a thumbnail, a title and video duration.

Fig. 2. Developed layouts presented to seniors in phase 1.

The second layout (Layout 2 - Fig. 2) was based on the Netflix interface, with horizontal navigation, similarly to layout 1, however containing a lot more information. In this layout proposal, the two video lists, for seen and unseen videos as shown in the first layout, are condensed to the bottom half of the screen, in order to include a main section previewing the content of the videos. This section provides more details about the selected video, specifically title, description, duration, thumbnail and how long ago the video was created.

Lastly, layout 3 (Fig. 2) is a variation of layout 1 where the navigation is done vertically instead of horizontally. In this proposal, each list only shows two cards on the screen, which leaves room to include more information, including date and a larger font-sized title.

The main goal of this phase was to understand which of these navigation typologies, vertical or horizontal, was best suited for the project's target demographic and what kind of information was most relevant to be displayed.

To conclude which of the three video library layouts was preferred by seniors, an experiment with a restricted number of participants was conducted. Each layout represents a way of presenting information and navigating through it.

The sample for this study's phase consisted of four participants, 50% males and 50% females, all of them over 65 years old and students at Senior University of Curia - Portugal. They were selected via convenience sampling due to the difficulty of selecting a random sample. The participants were already familiar with the project, since they had already been involved in previous data collections, where other visual elements of the iTV platform were defined [12]. Each participant had the opportunity of navigating through each one of the proposed layouts so that the choice of the preferred one would be based on actual user experience and not solely on expectation. This experiment was divided in two parts, an individual Cognitive Walkthrough followed by a focus group with the four participants. The Cognitive Walkthrough, described by Wharton et al. [13], is considered a very effective usability inspection method to apply during the design and development process of a technological solution. With this analytical technique, a sequence of actions should be performed by the user to complete the designated task, included in a list of tasks requested by the responsible researcher.

The Cognitive Walkthrough would start with the investigator contextualizing the user about the experiment and, subsequently, it was explained to the participants that they would be able to interact with three distinct layout proposals for the video library.

Prior to this more effective phase, the researcher talked with all the participants about trivialities to create a more relaxed environment. After testing the three interfaces, each participant would be asked to wait in a room while the other participants finished their tests. Afterwards, all the participants were gathered in the testing room to start the focus group and then encouraged to share their opinions regarding their experience. In the end, they were required to choose their preferred layout, which needed to be a group decision.

3.2 Usability Evaluation

After the participants selected the video library interface that most appealed to them in the first phase, the chosen design was implemented to the high-fidelity prototype of the platform, which led to a posterior second phase of tests, focused on the overall system's usability.

Thus, the second phase consisted in testing usability of a high-fidelity prototype of the platform through an observational study with potential end users. These tests were conducted by two members of the +TV4E research team and took place in an adult day care center in Aveiro, Portugal.

The participants included in this study were selected by convenience among seniors integrated in an adult day care center in Aveiro city. For the sample selection, the considered inclusion criteria were: being over 60 years old; watching television regularly; knowing how to read and providing an informed consent. Exclusion criteria were all the other conditions or circumstances which could compromise the subject's ability to take part in the study. The number of elderly participants included in the sample was 11, namely seven women (63.6%) and four men (36.4%). The participants had an average age of 84.8 years (SD = 7.35), with a maximum of 99 and a minimum of 69 years. The participants were invited to perform a list of previously defined tasks through a Cognitive Walkthrough method that was verbally explained by the responsible researcher. Simultaneously, a second researcher registered the participant's actions in a performance evaluation grid as well as observations/critical incidents occurred during each task in a specific area.

Each participant was invited to complete 14 tasks, previously defined in a task script and verbally explained by the responsible researcher, to offer the research team an overall view of the system's usability. While participants were performing the tasks, an observer registered quantitative data in a performance evaluation grid. For each task, the following data was observed: the success or failure in carrying out the task, the execution time (in seconds), the total number of errors and observations/critical incidents.

Although this test was focused on the usability of the system as a whole, in the context of this paper, only the tasks regarding the video library will be focused. Within the list of 14 tasks defined for system overall testing, tasks number 11, 12 and 13 were specifically related to video library interactions. The users were asked the following orientation regarding these three tasks: T11 (Access the video library) – press the key number "0"; T12 (Check how many videos are in the library sorted as viewed) – if applicable, explore the video library (through the d'pad buttons) and verbalize how many videos are in this feature classified as "viewed" video; T13 (Watch a video available in the library) – choose one video available and press the "ok" button to start the visualization.

Afterwards, the responsible researcher applied a Post-Study System Usability Questionnaire (PSSUQ) to test the usability of the high-fidelity prototype. The PSSUQ is a tool developed by the International Business Machines (IBM) to understand the user satisfaction regarding a system usability [14]. Rosa and colleagues [15] validated the PSSUQ to the European Portuguese version, with positive results of psychometric evaluation.

After the PSSUQ, a final questionnaire was applied to the participants in order to collect qualitative data concerning usefulness, aspects that should be improved and satisfaction levels. This questionnaire was previously defined, including open-ended questions for which the participant's answers were written down by the researcher.

3.3 Definition of the Final Layout

After collecting data during the second phase, it was clear that some key aspects in the video library feature should be improved to enhance the potential of this feature.

In line with this, it was developed a new layout for the video library, based in the state of the art review and in the results of phase 1, which showed that the best approach is a horizontal navigation list without video categorization. Beside this, strong colours were also adjusted. Previously, the text was pure black (hexadecimal colour value: #000000) and the background was almost white (hexadecimal colour value: ##FEFBF7), so they were replaced for softer tones (see Fig. 3) in order to soften the interface. It was added a subtle space between video cards to reduce visual weight and a soft blue stroke highlighting the selected video. These were adjustments focused on providing a simpler, softer and cleaner design to the library.

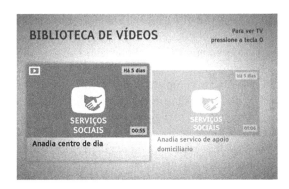

Fig. 3. Developed layout presented to seniors in phase 3. (Color figure online)

Similarly to phase 1, a focus group was conducted with four participants (one male and three females) with an average of 72 years old (SD = 5.4) and aimed to validate the best approach to the video library between the layout chosen back in phase 1 and the new layout (Fig. 3). All individuals included in the sample were students at Senior University of Curia – Portugal. This moment was guided by two members of the +TV4E research team, namely the responsible researcher and an observer. After the explanation of this moment's dynamics, the participants were invited to freely explore the two video library layouts. Simultaneously, the observer registered observations/critical incidents that occurred during the interaction.

The participants were asked some short questions regarding their experience, which helped gather individual opinions from each participant before having them discussing their opinions during the focus group. The questions were made in the following order (during the focus group): (1) In which of the templates was more difficult to find a video?; (2) If you want to watch a video, which of the templates would you like to use? (3) Do you consider that categorizing the videos is important/useful?; (4) which of the templates was more useful and comfortable to use?.

In the end, the responsible researcher required the participants to choose their preferred layout, which needed to be a group decision.

4 Results and Discussion

The main results achieved in the several phases are presented below.

4.1 Video Library Design (Phase 1)

The phase 1 wielded both individual results for each participant and a group decision for the best overall interface layout. The individual results are synthetized in Table 1 and include all the suggestions that users made during the several components of the design phase (see Figs. 1, 2 and 3).

Table 1. Individual opinions' for each layout (phase 1)

	Layout 1	Layout 2	Layout 3
Subject 1	The video cards are easy to distinguish since the title occupies less space	The selected video is not big enough. The lighter colours are not distinguishable	The background colour cannot be distinguished from the cards
Subject 2	The play symbol should be blinking to make it clear that it plays the video	Headers should be bigger. The font should be changed or have a different colour	Vertical navigation is better than horizontal. Having two cards per column is appropriate since they are bigger
Subject 3	Liked it because it was simple and easy to navigate. Should have less cards shown on screen	Has too much information. Should have less cards shown on screen	Easy to understand which card is selected. Two cards per column makes it easy to read
Subject 4	Duration of the video is important to keep. Intuitive navigation	Too much information makes the layout confusing. Number of thumbnails is appropriate	Prefers horizontal navigation

Regarding each of the participant's individual preference, all participants with the exception of participant 2 chose layout 1 as their favourite.

Since most participants had already chosen layout 1, the focus group results were very similar to the individual results. In the end, the majority of the participants preferred layout 1, since it featured horizontal navigation and fewer interface elements. The participants justified this by saying they were already familiar with the horizontal navigation, therefore making it easier to use. The focus group participants also decided that the appropriate number of video cards per list should be three, in order to allow them to be bigger and thus easier to read.

4.2 Usability Evaluation (Phase 2)

Almost all requested tasks were successfully performed and concluded by the participants in phase 2. However, analysing the performance evaluation grid it was notorious that tasks requiring interaction with the video library registered the lowest success rates. When participants were asked to interact with the video library interface, none of them could understand the concept of video library and how it worked.

The data recorded by the observer shows that, in T11 (Access the video library): several participants were very insecure and did not know/remember which key should have been pressed; many participants pressed other key numbers and the "OK" button and searched for a key labelled "video library". In task number 12 (Check how many videos are in the library sorted as viewed), several usability problems were detected, such as: people did not understand how the video library worked, especially the video categorization as "seen" and "unseen"; participants did not quite understand the layout arrangement of the components on the screen. Finally, in T13 (Watch a video available in the library) the participants did not understand which card was selected and how to navigate between videos/elements. These difficulties were reflected in the error rates.

One of the addressed features in the questionnaire survey was focused on the video library usefulness ("Do you think the video library is useful?"). In this question, nine participants (81.8%) considered this feature to be useful. Crossing this data with the information collected on the performance evaluation grid and in the PSSUQ, the research team realized that this feature can be very helpful for elderly, but the interface should be rethought and improved to become easier to use.

4.3   Definition of the Final Layout (Phase 3)

Regarding the results achieved in phase 2, another layout possibility was designed for the video library interface which was evaluated side by side with the previously chosen layout (Layout 1 vs Layout 4).

From the four participants included in the final phase, two of them had previously tested the +TV4E project, while the remaining two were exposed to the project for the first time. During the free exploration moment, when layout 1 was presented to the participants, all of them were able to switch between the video lists ("seen" and "unseen"), as well as to realize how many healthcare videos were in the library and to select a requested video. Despite this, when layout 4 was shown, the participants stated that this new propose was easier to navigate and considered it more attractive and easier to read due to the larger thumbnail size.

It was also easily perceived by the sample that the videos, classified as "seen" and "unseen" in layout 1, were mixed in a single line which was not considered a limitation in the interface use. Some participants recognized the benefit of separating the videos in two lists but globally preferred the simplicity of having all videos in one list sorted by date.

In the end, the elected interface by unanimity was layout 4. This choice was justified by the larger scale of the elements which improved readability and its simplicity, since it only requires horizontal navigation.

5   Conclusions and Future Work

Developing technologies that cater to needs of seniors is paramount to promote their quality of life. Quality of life can be measured in terms of independence from their informal networks, such as, the informative dependence from their caregivers and dependence while doing day-to-day activities, such as shopping, eating and dressing.

The aim of this study was to define the best interface for a video library feature to integrate in the final +TV4E prototype. This process proved to be complex concerning the difficulty of recruiting participants to integrate the process in order to define the video library, as well as the perception what entails in practice to choose one of the layouts. It is known that the number of participants in the sample is limited, however, it was considered sufficient to obtain guidelines to define the improvement points of the platform.

At the end of this evolutionary study was considered successful since the participants clearly understood the purpose of the tests carried out and it was possible to get a decision between all of them.

Following the final choice of layout 4, this feature was integrated into +TV4E project iTV application and it is being evaluated at the moment as part of another ongoing +TV4E study. This study is being carried out in a domestic environment with real context users and has the goal of testing the first iteration of the application as a whole.

One of the main contributions of this work is related with the data collection methods when working with older people. It is difficult to predict the participants' reactions, answers or behaviours when trying to define a data collection tool, however, the ability to adapt the process in the simplest way is essential to obtain good quality data. Despite this, seniors' participation in the design and development process of the video library leads to a better efficiency of the final product, which amplifies the possibility in having a technological solution able to answer end-users' needs and expectations.

In conclusion, this study appraised the need to involve seniors in the development process of platforms and showed that, occasionally, it is not easy to achieve final decisions in a single interaction moment.

Acknowledgements. The research leading to this work has received funding from Project 3599 – Promover a Produção Científica e Desenvolvimento Tecnológico e a Constituição de Redes Temáticas (3599-PPCDT) and European Commission Funding FEDER (through FCT: Fundação para a Ciência e Tecnologia I.P. under grant agreement no. PTDC/IVC-COM/3206/2014).

References

1. United Nations: World Population Prospects: The 2017 Revision, Key Findings and Advance Tables, New York, USA (2017)
2. Vechiato, F.L., Vidotti, S.A.B.G.: Recomendações de usabilidade e de acessibilidade em projetos de ambientes informacionais digitais para idosos. Tendências da Pesqui. Bras. em Ciência da Informação, p. 5 (2012)
3. Hernández-Encuentra, E., Pousada, M., Gómez-Zúñiga, B.: ICT and older people: beyond usability. Educ. Gerontol. **35**, 226–245 (2009). https://doi.org/10.1080/03601270802466934
4. Campelo, D., Silva, T., Abreu, J.: Recommending personalized informative contents on iTV. In: Adjunct Publication of the 2017 ACM International Conference on Interactive Experiences for TV and Online Video (TVX 2017 Adjunct), pp. 99–103. ACM, New York (2017). https://doi.org/10.1145/3084289.3084292
5. Instituto Nacional de Estatística: Projeções de População Residente 2015–2080 (2017)
6. Kalache, A., Gatti, A.: Active ageing: a policy framework (2002)
7. Silva, T., Abreu, J., Antunes, M., Almeida, P., Silva, V., Santinha, G.: +TV4E: interactive television as a support to push information about social services to the elderly. In: Procedia Computer Science, vol. 100, pp. 580–585 (2016). ISSN 1877-0509
8. Caravau, H., Silva, T., Silva, V.: Interrupt emission or ask if TV viewer wants to see. In: 2017 12th Iberian Conference on Information Systems and Technologies (CISTI), Lisbon, pp. 1–6 (2017). https://doi.org/10.23919/cisti.2017.7975753

9. Rosenberg, P., Ross, A., Garçon, L.: WHO Global Forum on Innovations for Ageing Populations, Kobe, Japan (2013)
10. Reis, L., Caravau, H., Silva, T., Almeida, P.: Automatic creation of TV content to integrate in seniors viewing activities. In: Abásolo, M.J., Almeida, P., Pina Amargós, J. (eds.) jAUTI 2016. CCIS, vol. 689, pp. 32–46. Springer, Cham (2017). https://doi.org/10.1007/978-3-319-63321-3_3
11. Mota, M., Caravau, H., Silva, T.: Designing a video library for senior users of iTV. In: 6th Iberoamerican Conference on Applications and Usability of Interactive TV (jAUTI 2017), Aveiro, Portugal, 12–13 October 2017
12. Silva, T., Caravau, H., Reis, L., Almeida, P.: Iconography's development for a seniors' iTV informative platform. In: Procedia Computer Science, vol. 121, pp. 576–583 (2017). ISSN 1877-0509, https://doi.org/10.1016/j.procs.2017.11.076
13. Wharton, C., Rieman, J., Lewis, C., Polson, P.: The cognitive walkthrough method: a practitioner's guide. In: Nielson, J., Mack, R. (eds.) Usability Inspection Methods, pp. 105–140. Wiley, New York (1994)
14. Lewis, J.R.: Psychometric evaluation of the PSSUQ using data from five years of usability studies. Int. J. Hum. Comput. Interact. **14**, 463–488 (2002). https://doi.org/10.1177/154193129203601617
15. Rosa, A.F., Martins, A.I., Costa, V., Queirós, A., Silva, A., Rocha, N.P.: European Portuguese validation of the post-study system usability questionnaire (PSSUQ). In: 2015 10th Iberian Conference on Information Systems and Technologies (CISTI). IEEE (2015)

Automatic View Tracking in 360º Multimedia Using xAPI

Antoni Oliver(✉) ⃝, Javier del Molino ⃝, and Antoni Bibiloni ⃝

Laboratorio de Tecnologías de la Información Multimedia (LTIM),
Departamento de Matemáticas e Informática,
Universitat de les Illes Balears, Palma, Spain
{antoni.oliver,toni.bibiloni}@uib.es,
j.delmolino1@estudiant.uib.es

Abstract. 360º video can consume up to six times the bandwidth of a regular video by delivering the entire frames instead of just the current viewport, introducing an additional difficulty to the delivery of this kind of multimedia. Many authors address this challenge by narrowing the delivered viewport using knowledge of where the user is likely to look at. To address this, we propose an automatic view tracking system based in xAPI to collect the data required to create the knowledge required to decide the viewport that is going to be delivered. We present a use case of an interactive 360º video documentary around the migratory crisis in Greece. In this case, omnidirectional content is recorded using a 6-camera array, rendered in an equirectangular projection and played later by an HTML5 web application. Interactive hotspots are placed on specific coordinates of the space-time of the production, introducing a connection of the viewer with the story by playing additional multimedia content. The current view and other usage data are recorded and permit us to obtain metrics on the user behavior, like most watched areas, with the goal to obtain that required knowledge.

Keywords: Hypervideo · 360º video · Interactive documentary · Video tiling
View-adaptive streaming · xAPI

1   Introduction

360º videos have greatly grown in popularity recently thanks to the introduction of this kind of multimedia by major video social networks Youtube and Facebook. To consume this kind of videos on a web browser, several types of interfaces can be used to select the desired viewport. Popular choices include a drag interface (using either a pointing device or touches on a screen) or a sensor-enabled device, like a smartphone or a head-mounted display (HMD).

All these interfaces work by selecting a portion of the 360º viewport to be displayed at the users' choice. To be able to display that portion in a reasonable quality, the original video needs to be encoded in a very high resolution. This results in a very large bandwidth usage, of which only a rough 8% is displayed as the selected viewport.

© Springer International Publishing AG, part of Springer Nature 2018
M. J. Abásolo et al. (Eds.): jAUTI 2017, CCIS 813, pp. 117–131, 2018.
https://doi.org/10.1007/978-3-319-90170-1_9

To address this misusage, a number of approaches are suggested in the literature to reduce the delivered amount of information, most of them revolved around trying to predict where the user is going to view at and assign less (if any) bitrate to the area outside of that predicted viewport.

In this paper we introduce a method to automatically record the position at which the user is looking at when watching a 360° video. We demonstrate the feasibility of this approach through a use case of an interactive 360° video documentary that, following the structure of a hypervideo, depicts the situation of the refugees that flee from war and arrive in Greece since 2015.

This section includes a revision of the current state of the art in interactive multimedia, VR videos and how the literature addresses their bandwidth usage. Section 2 reviews previous work on which this method is based, including the tools needed to create and play the 360° documentary and automatically record the viewport watched by the users. Section 3 explains how to collect this data using xAPI, represent it using heatmaps and how we propose to analyze that data to be used to reduce the bandwidth used by this kind of videos. Finally, the conclusion can be found in Sect. 4, where we also talk about the future work.

1.1   State of the Art

A hypervideo is a navigable stream of video that offers the viewer the possibility of choosing a path in the narrative combining several multimedia tracks through spatial and temporal links present in the media [1]. We extend this concept to support 360° media, including links around the sphere of the 360° panorama. Interactive documentaries have been analyzed in [2], encouraging users to explore and navigate the production, rather than simply viewing it.

Bleumers et al. introduce the users' expectations of omnidirectional video in [3]. 360° multimedia belongs to the field of Virtual Reality (VR) [4, 5]. This field has traditionally made use of several gadgets and devices to create an immersive experience, like head-mounted displays (HMD) or the CAVE [6]. Despite this, there is an increasing trend to display 360° video in an interactive scene inside web browsers in desktop and mobile devices, given the recent adoption of this novel medium by popular online video platforms, like YouTube[1] or Facebook[2], that have begun offering immersive 360° video upload and visualization services. This is thanks to the ability to display a 3D scene to project the equirectangular video texture inside the browser itself since the introduction of WebGL[3], in 2011. The current state of 360° video playback is shared between HMD like the Oculus Rift[4] and web-based navigation in video services like the ones mentioned before, featuring a desktop drag-and-drop interface and a sensor-enabled view for smartphones. In the literature,

---

[1] https://youtube-creators.googleblog.com/2015/03/a-new-way-to-see-and-share-your-world.html.

[2] https://facebook360.fb.com.

[3] https://www.khronos.org/webgl/.

[4] https://www.oculus.com/.

omnidirectional lectures were given using HMD [7], a drag interface for 360° hyper-video is presented in [8], and more recently Augmented Reality has been introduced in smartphones [9].

Regarding the representation of the users' actions inside a 360° video, commercial solutions like Wistia[5] or LiveHEAT[6] use heatmaps to show the area in the 3D space that is watched by the users. Similar techniques are used in the literature [10, 11].

Finally, to reduce the bandwidth consumed when streaming VR videos, current research strives in identifying the viewport that is going to be displayed so that bandwidth can be saved, or additional bit rate can be assigned to the areas that are actually displayed, resulting in a form of viewport-adaptive streaming. It is unthinkable not using some sort of adaptive streaming at this point; most of the initiatives in the literature are based on MPEG-DASH [12]. [13, 14] performed an experiment with a HMD in which they recorded the users' motion. Using neural networks, they demonstrate that motion prediction is feasible within 0.1 and 0.5 s, achieving a reduction of bandwidth of more than 40% and a failure ratio of under 0.1% with a prediction window of 0.2 s. Other authors make use of what is called *frame tiling*, consisting in dividing the omnidirectional frames in a matrix of tiles, which are requested by the client specifically: [15] propose a tiled streaming scheme over cellular networks, achieving theoretical bandwidth savings of up to 80%; [16] present a system based on HMDs that leverages MPEG-DASH SRD [17] to describe the spatial relationship of the tiles in the 360° space; [18] study how the choice of the projection mapping (equirectangular, cubemap, pyramid, dodecahedron), the length of the segments and the number of representations impact the viewport quality, concluding that the cubemap projection, segments of 2 s and between 5 and 7 representations achieves the best quality with a given budget bit rate. Facebook has been researching this topic since 2016: they first proposed [19] the use of a pyramidal projection, that is dependent on the view, to achieve reductions of up to 80% at the expense of creating 30 different representations of the same media. These are pre-generated and stored. A year later, they optimized [20] dynamic streaming decreasing bit rates by up to 92% and decreasing interruptions by more than 80% by introducing offset cubemaps. After that, they seek [21] to further enhance the experience by using a predicted position instead of the current one, using a prediction system based on a heatmap of the most popular zones of every frame. Since this heatmap alone does not suffice to provide an accurate prediction, they create a gravitational predictor from that, creating valleys in a sphere that correspond to most viewed areas. The position of the user is affected by the geography using a physics simulator, resulting in local influence for point of interest (PoI) and the ability to escape of that influence with strong enough kinetic momentum.

---

[5] https://wistia.com/.

[6] http://www.finwe.mobi/main/liveheat/.

2   The Interactive 360° Documentary

Over a million people have arrived in Greece since 2015. Refugees flee from war horrors and dreadful armed conflicts. Babies, children and elderly people are especially vulnerable. Migrants arrive and will be still arriving while conflicts last.[7]

In collaboration with PROEM-AID[8], a group of emergency professionals who voluntarily help in Greece, the team recorded 360° footage in the refugee camp and, together with additional, regular video content, prepared a use case for a novel format of interactive documentaries, letting the user to explore a 360° video and obtain additional information in the form of audiovisual content at their request.

We propose the following format for describing an interactive experience with a 360° video: a main video track plays as a panorama, allowing the user to pan the scene and look at any direction. This track serves as a common thread for additional media that is linked to specific points in the space-time of the main track. In these moments, a marker is displayed in the scene, linking to a follow-up video of what is seen in the main track.

This format is based on [22], allowing us to automatically record the user behavior (video controls such as play, pause; 360° controls and also interaction controls, in the form of the selection of a point of interest), especially keeping track of the users' view position at any given moment.

In this section we review how this production was created, by recording the raw images in situ and editing them, how these videos are turned into an interactive experience and how the final product is displayed in the viewers' web browsers, by following Fig. 1. We invite the readers to visit the web application at http://ltim.uib.es/proemaid.

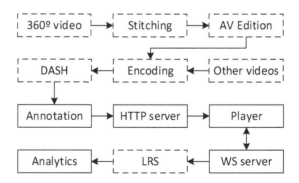

Fig. 1. General overview.

---

[7] Adapted from http://www.proemaid.org/en/lesbos/.

[8] http://www.proemaid.org/en/.

2.1 Recording and Editing

Two kinds of footage were recorded in the refugee camps in Lesvos and Piraeus, Greece: the 360° media and several linear clips. Four 360° scenes of approximately 90 s each were captured using a 6-camera array, placed on a stick. The media was stitched using Kolor's Autopano Video Pro[9], obtaining an equirectangular clip.

Since both the equirectangular and the linear clips were recorded using high bit rates, not easily supported by most network conditions, they were encoded following the MPEG DASH standard [12] into multiple bit rates. This resulted in several multimedia files and the MPD file for each multimedia file, including the 360° one.

2.2 Introducing the Interactivity

The process of creating the interactive production from the main 360° video track and multiple linear video files is supported by a web application that generates the metadata needed to display the markers.

This annotation tool provides an interactive interface to edit the list of positions that this marker takes in the 360° video. The user is able to navigate the media to select a desired position in space and time to place one of these key positions. This application is designed and built with React[10], and makes use of a scene component to preview and place the key positions of the markers that is also included in the player.

The representation of the positions of a given point of interest is a sequence of points (at least two) in the space-time of the 360° video track, where t is the time in seconds; δ is the latitude in degrees from the equator of the scene; and λ is the longitude in degrees from the meridian zero of the equirectangular frame (see (1) and Fig. 2).

$$(t_0, \delta_0, \lambda_0), \dots, (t_N, \delta_N, \lambda_N) \tag{1}$$

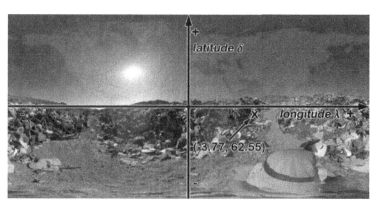

Fig. 2. Notation of latitude and longitude in the equirectangular frame

---

[9] http://www.kolor.com/autopano-video/.
[10] https://facebook.github.io/react/.

The additional metadata for each point of interest includes a descriptive name, an IRI (Internationalized Resource Identifier) to identify that point, the IRI of the video that should play when selected and an optional image to customize the marker that appears in the scene. This information is stored in a JSON file and retrieved by the player.

2.3   Playing the Production in a Web Browser

Once the interactive 360° video has been defined, it can be played in a WebGL enabled browser. The player is also a web application built with React, and it recycles the same scene component included in the editor to display the 360° video. This time, the extra functionalities of this scene are enabled: the video controls, the marker help area and all events are actually listened (see Fig. 3).

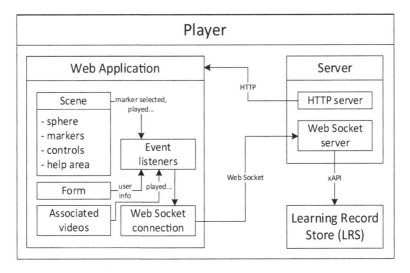

Fig. 3. Architecture of the interactive 360° video player environment.

Before playing the production, a form prompts the user to share some personal information (gender, age, profession, country) with us, so we will be able to obtain some statistics by this information.

By listening these events, the player is notified when a marker is selected, so its associated video will play in a pop-up view, interrupting the main track playback. When this video ends or the user closes the pop-up view, the main playback continues.

A Web Socket connection is established with the server keeping track of these events, which are stored in an LRS thanks to xAPI.

Every video file in this production has been encoded at multiple bit rates. In the player side, the MPD manifests are loaded by the DASH.js[11] JavaScript player and, when the media starts playing, it automatically adapts its bit rate.

---

[11] https://github.com/Dash-Industry-Forum/dash.js/.

The 3D scene. This component, shared by the editor and the player, houses a WebGL scene managed by Three.js. The core of this scene is the sphere used to display the frames of the 360° texture provided by the main equirectangular video track. This component is provided the list of points of interest, from which circles are created in their respective positions, firing an event when selected. That position is calculated via linear interpolation in spherical coordinates using Ed William's aviation formula[12].

$$f = \frac{t - t_0}{t_1 - t_0}$$

$$d = \cos^{-1}\left[\cos \delta_0 \cos \delta_1 \cos\left(\lambda_0 - \lambda_1\right) + \sin \delta_0 \sin \delta_1\right]$$

$$A = \frac{\sin\left(1 - f\right)d}{\sin d}$$

$$B = \frac{\sin f \cdot d}{\sin d}$$

$$p_t = R\begin{bmatrix} A \cos \delta_0 \cos \lambda_0 + B \cos \delta_1 \cos \lambda_1 \\ A \sin \delta_0 + B \sin \delta_1 \\ A \cos \delta_0 \sin \lambda_0 + B \cos \delta_1 \sin \lambda_1 \end{bmatrix} \qquad (2)$$

For a particular time t, $t_0 \le t \le t_1$, and knowing two key positions at t_0 and t_1, $\left(t_0, \delta_0, \lambda_0\right)$ and $\left(t_1, \delta_1, \lambda_1\right)$, the position p_t in Cartesian coordinates for that marker in that time at a distance of R is obtained via (2).

To be able to detect when a marker is selected, intersections are looked for with a ray casted from the camera position to the selected position. Other events are fired when play conditions change, that will be used by the component that includes the scene, either the editor or the player.

Additional parameters can be passed to the scene to enable two player-specific features: the controls to adjust playback of the 360° video, featuring a progress bar that hints the times when points of interest appear and a help area that displays again the markers that are shown somewhere in the scene, so the user can still see them if they are outside the camera's field of view (see Fig. 4).

Usage tracking. The events fired by the scene are listened by the player and then forwarded via a Web Socket connection to the server. Instead of collecting all the data and submitting it in the end, this approach was chosen to permit us to visualize in real time the users' actions. Once this information is received by the server, it is stored into the LRS via xAPI.

xAPI[13] is a simple but powerful mechanism to store and retrieve logs and share them with any imaginable system. It is a Representational State Transfer (RESTful) API in

---

[12] http://edwilliams.org/avform.htm#Intermediate.
[13] https://experienceapi.com/.

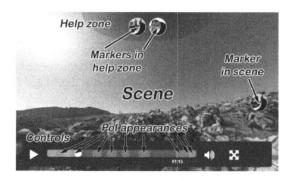

Fig. 4. User interface of the interactive player, featuring the markers in the scene, the help zone with its markers and the controls with its PoI appearances.

which any statement of experience (it can happen anywhere and on any platform) can be tracked as a record. Any kind of experience can be tracked, although xAPI was developed with learning experiences in mind.

A statement is a simple construct, written in JavaScript Object Notation (JSON) format, to store an aspect of an experience consisting of, at a minimum, three parts: an actor, a verb and an object. A set of several statements, each representing an event in time, can be used to track complete details about an experience: its quantity may depend on the need for more or less detail in later reporting.

A Learning Record Store (LRS) is the heart of xAPI, because it receives, stores and returns data about the defined experiences.

The following text extends Table 1, that describes the relation between events and statement verbs. The vocabulary used in this application is based on ADL's video vocabulary [23] and on the general xAPI vocabulary registry [24]. Additional vocabulary has been created and submitted to the general registry.

Table 1. Relation between events and xAPI statement verb IRIs

Event	Verb
The form is submitted	https://w3id.org/xapi/adl/verbs/logged-in
A video track is ready	http://adlnet.gov/expapi/verbs/initialized
A video track is played	https://w3id.org/xapi/video/verbs/played
A video track is paused	https://w3id.org/xapi/video/verbs/paused
A video track is sought	https://w3id.org/xapi/video/verbs/seeked
A video track ends	https://w3id.org/xapi/video/verbs/completed
The main video track is navigated	https://ltim.uib.es/xapi/verbs/lookedat
A marker is selected	http://id.tincanapi.com/verb/selected
The associated video is closed	https://w3id.org/xapi/video/verbs/terminated
The user closes the player	http://id.tincanapi.com/verb/abandoned

The actor for these statements is specified either with using their e-mail address, if provided, or a version 4 UUID as the name of a local account, to deal with anonymous users. The *logged-in* statement is sent to store the users' personal information. Just after that, an *initialized* statement is submitted specifying the main video's IRI, creating a video session from its ID, according to the video vocabulary.

The *played*, *paused*, *seeked* and *completed* statements are used according to the video vocabulary, attaching the following video extensions: *session-id*, *quality*, *screen-size*, *user-agent*, *volume*, *video-playback-size* and *time* (or *time-from* and *time-to*, in the case of a *seeked* statement, refer [23]). An additional extension is defined: https://ltim.uib.es/xapi/extensions/orientation, containing an object with the current view's latitude and longitude.

Following the same design, the *looked at* statement is submitted when the user changes the current view. Successive submissions are throttled to 250 ms so as not to flood the LRS. In this case, *orientation-from* and *orientation-to* are used instead of the *orientation* extension, following the design of the *seeked* statement with *time*.

The *selected* statement is sent to the LRS whenever a point of interest is selected through its marker. This statement includes the additional data present in the *played* statement as context extensions and the IRI of the point of interest as a result extension. From this moment, the associated video window opens, and it begins to load. When it does, an *initialized* statement is generated following the previous behavior, but specifying an object definition type of https://w3id.org/xapi/video/activity-type/video and still using the previous *initialized* statement ID as its *session-id*.

As it is natural, the user is free to interact with the associated video, and *played*, *paused*, *seeked* and *completed* statements will be generated much like previously specified, but with the following differences: the object definition type changes, as in this second *initialized* statement; this second *initialized* statement's ID is used as the *session-id* and the *orientation* extension is unused.

Whenever the user closes the associated video's window, a *terminated* statement is stored in the LRS, including the same additional data these previous statements would. This marks the end of the session of an associated video.

Finally, when the user closes the player, an abandoned statement is submitted, marking the end of the session.

3   Results

After sufficient users have played the 360° video, the LRS contains lots of valuable data that needs to be analyzed; at the time of this writing, over 300 sessions are stored. This section describes the process to retrieve a preliminary set of data from the LRS, the analysis performed on that data and our proposal of actuation from the knowledge gained from this experience. Bokeh[14] version 0.12.13 was used to generate the interactive graphs shown in the following figures.

---

[14] https://bokeh.pydata.org/en/latest/.

3.1 Data Retrieval

Statements may be fetched from the LRS using standard methods prescribed by xAPI. A big advantage is that we do not need to know how the multimedia player works internally, so the information gets ready in the LRS to be digested at any time by any external system. For complex reporting, all relevant statements can be moved into a data warehouse to be processed later. Although, for simple reporting, metrics can be directly obtained from these statements (this is the approach we have chosen).

It is possible to analyze this information to discover trends, obtain measurements, perform evaluations, comparisons or tracking, or create validation reports on user experiences. A preliminary set of results have been obtained so far from the data collected in the LRS using xAPI, detailed next.

For example, in Fig. 5, two complementary graphs are drawn with data coming from three different 360° video sessions (each session has its own color). They are complementary because the same information is represented in both graphs (with different coordinates). The graph on the left represents playback time versus longitude. Dashed gray lines are superposed to help us know where the markers are displayed in the scene. The graph on the right represents playback time versus relative timestamp: relative to the initialized statement, to be able to coherently compare different sessions.

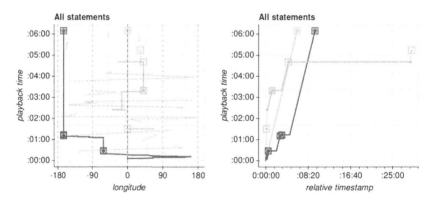

Fig. 5. Statements generated during three sessions. (Color figure online)

Solid lines indicate that the video track was played, was navigated or was paused (not filled squares indicate the moment when the video was paused). Dotted lines indicate that it was sought. Circles indicate the moment when a marker was selected (and an associated video was played, partially at least): filled circles are used the first time the marker was selected, and not filled circles are used the following times. Asterisks indicate the moment when the video was completed. Any session starts at longitude 0°, as the left graph represents.

These graphs allow us to observe, very quickly, how a user has interacted with the video: if they have made left and right movements (the graph on the left tells us exactly where), if they have paused the video (the graph on the right tells us exactly how long), if they have selected markers (and which ones), if they have sought to a new point (the graph on the right tells us if a student has watched all the video content or just made jumps over it until they have reached the end), etc.

For example, in the particular case of Fig. 5:

- The green session corresponds to a user whose attention has not been grabbed by the interactivity offered by the activity: they have only played the 360° video from the beginning, nothing else.
- The dark blue session corresponds to a user that has moved left and right during the first 20 s, until they have played an associated video. Then they have continued watching the 360° video, without interacting with it, during about 40 s, followed by new movements before another associated video has been played twice. No more interactions come later and the 360° video has been watched until the end.
- The pale blue session corresponds to a user not interested in the beginning of the activity: they have directly sought to second 90 (:01:30), where they moved for a while, with the 360° video still paused, followed by a new jump to second 140 (: 02:20), where new movements have been made. Then they have watched the 360° video, without interacting with it, during nearly 60 s, followed by some movements until they have watched an associated video. Later, they have watched the 360° video, without interacting with it, during about 80 s, at which moment they have paused the activity for around 25 min, with some movements in the meantime. Finally, they have sought to second 310 (:05:10) and have skipped the rest of the activity.

3.2 360° Navigation Analysis

We have just shown one of the many possible results that can be obtained from user interactions stored in the LRS, which starts to unveil the potential of this platform.

Heatmaps become another possibility, very useful to show the spatial distribution of statements generated by a subset of users. For this example, in which we are interested in the most frequently selected viewports, we will draw the location distribution of continuous paths: only *played* and *looked at* statements.

This kind of histogram is built from its equivalent playback time versus longitude graph (like the one on the left in Fig. 5), as follows:

1. The plane is divided into a grid of bins (each bin has the same width and height as the rest of the bins).
2. We assign the value 0 to each bin.
3. Solid segments (corresponding to *played* and *looked at* statements in its equivalent playback time versus longitude graph Fig. 5) are sampled following the created grid.
4. We add 1 to the value corresponding to any bin containing a segment.

The graphs in Fig. 6 represent two heatmaps of continuous paths (playback time versus longitude) for 10 independent sessions: the darker the color, the higher the quantity of statements present in the area delimited by each bin. Both graphs represent the same 10 sessions, but the left graph has 9 × 9 bins (each bin has width 40° and height 41 s) and the right graph has 25 × 25 bins (each bin has width 14.4° and height 14.8 s). The number of bins is customizable, of course.

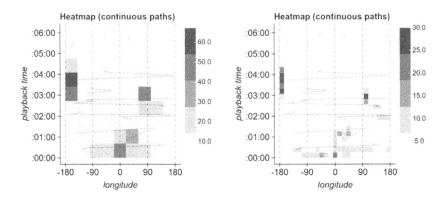

Fig. 6. Heatmaps of continuous paths corresponding to ten sessions.

Dashed gray lines are superposed (in the same way as in the left graph of Fig. 5) denoting the position of markers: we can thus compare how the statements are distributed around selectable objects. The graph on the left can give us a general insight of which zones have been more or less visited by users, whereas the graph on the right is able to refine them more. Depending on the actual need, one or the other could be used (or both of them). As expected, it is clear that around coordinates (0, 0), where the activity always begins, a lot of continuous paths exist.

3.3 Proposal of Actuation

The results of playing the 360° video contribute to create a richer set of data that produces a more accurate heatmap, representing the areas of the scene that are more likely to appear in the viewport when playing the video again.

This information can be exploited, as seen in the literature, to condition the quality at which the video file is encoded. Following the state of the art, the VR video will be encoded in different quality settings for a given budget bit rate. Currently, the video is encoded in 4 different bit rates and the source to be played is chosen following the MPEG DASH specification. We propose to still have a number of bit rate configurations available, but a number of different representations of each of these will be created. These representations will be encoded assigning more bit rate to a particular area of the 360° scene, using one of the approaches suggested in the literature: equirectangular tiling, pyramidal mapping, offset cube maps, etc. To be able to play this complex video structure, modifications will be applied to the MPEG-DASH player that not only will choose a version according to the available bit rate, but also a representation according to the predicted position the user is going to center their viewport during the next period, so that predicted position is adjusted again, and a new representation is fetched.

4   Conclusion

The work presented in this document is an extension of the state of the art in interactive documentaries, introducing user-navigable 360° video and interaction in the form of additional videos that give further details about a specific topic. A use case was conducted with 360° and linear video footage in the refugee camps in Lesvos and Piraeus, which resulted in an interactive web application available to the public. Precise user interactions, including the tracking of the viewport in the 360° space, are logged in real time and analyzed to comprehend their decisions and navigation choices in this novel format. The web application is accessible at http://ltim.uib.es/proemaid.

Knowing (almost) everything the user does with the application enables us to perform very accurate monitoring of their behavior. Simply by observing the proposed graphs we can detected, in a moment, in what proportion users watch the 360° video, both in time and in position: if a video is linearly played or if users like to move inside the 360° environment (and to what extent: if they navigate around markers or if they navigate randomly).

Being able to obtain the information related to the selection of viewport performed by a preliminary set of data permitted us to create visualizations of that choice in the space-time of the 360° production, advancing us to our goal of reducing the bandwidth wasted by this kind of multimedia applications. The method based on xAPI we explained in this paper and previously introduced in [22] resulted adequate for the task and we expect the information it will generate will guide us into our objective. xAPI not only completely fulfills our logging needs, with the help of the LRS, but it also allows that different systems (not even developed by us) are able to talk to each other, thanks to its open interface.

Further enhancements are planned for the system, designing a mobile specific interface, using the device sensors and enabling the use of VR technologies like Oculus Rift and even Google Cardboard. It will be interesting to assess whether different interfaces need similar solutions to address their bandwidth usage.

We expect that we can achieve a significant bandwidth reduction by implementing a view-adaptive system based on the state of the art and refining its parameters for different user interfaces with the help of the automatic viewport tracking system we demonstrated in this paper.

Acknowledgements. The authors want to thank the people that appear in the documentary for sharing their stories with us. We also want to thank PROEM-AID for their work where they are much needed, and especially Manuel Elviro Vidal for recording the scenes shown in the documentary *in situ*. A. Oliver was supported by a predoctoral contract with the Universitat de les Illes Balears (UIB).

References

1. Sawhney, N., Balcom, D., Smith, I.: HyperCafe. In: Proceedings of the Seventh ACM Conference on Hypertext – HYPERTEXT 1996, pp. 1–10. ACM Press, New York (1996)

2. Gaudenzi, S.: The living documentary: from representing reality to co-creating reality in digital interactive documentary (2013)
3. Bleumers, L., Van den Broeck, W., Lievens, B., Pierson, J.: Seeing the bigger picture. In: Proceedings of the 10th European Conference on Interactive TV and Video – EuroiTV 2012, p. 115 (2012)
4. Sherman, W.R., Craig, A.B.: Understanding Virtual Reality: Interface, Application, and Design. Morgan Kaufmann, Los Altos (2003)
5. Neumann, U., Pintaric, T., Rizzo, A.: Immersive panoramic video. In: Proceedings of the Eighth ACM International Conference on Multimedia - MULTIMEDIA 2000, pp. 493–494. ACM Press, New York (2000)
6. Lantz, E.: The future of virtual reality. In: Proceedings of the 23rd Annual Conference on Computer Graphics and Interactive Techniques – SIGGRAPH 1996, pp. 485–486. ACM Press, New York (1996)
7. Kavanagh, S., Luxton-Reilly, A., Wüensche, B., Plimmer, B.: Creating 360° educational video. In: Proceedings of the 28th Australian Conference on Computer-Human Interaction – OzCHI 2016, pp. 34–39. ACM Press, New York (2016)
8. Neng, L.A.R., Chambel, T.: Get around 360° hypervideo. In: Proceedings of the 14th International Academic MindTrek Conference on Envisioning Future Media Environments – MindTrek 2010, p. 119. ACM Press, New York (2010)
9. Berning, M., Yonezawa, T., Riedel, T., Nakazawa, J., Beigl, M., Tokuda, H.: pARnorama. In: Proceedings of the 2013 ACM Conference on Pervasive and Ubiquitous Computing Adjunct Publication – UbiComp 2013 Adjunct, pp. 1471–1474. ACM Press, New York (2013)
10. Kasahara, S., Nagai, S., Rekimoto, J.: JackIn Head: immersive visual telepresence system with omnidirectional wearable camera. IEEE Trans. Vis. Comput. Graph. **23**, 1222–1234 (2017)
11. Williamson, J.R., Sundén, D., Bradley, J.: GlobalFestival: evaluating real world interaction on a spherical display. In: Proceedings of the Joint International Conference on Pervasive and Ubiquitous Computing, International Symposium on Wearable Computers, pp. 1251–1261 (2015)
12. Sodagar, I.: The MPEG-DASH standard for multimedia streaming over the internet. IEEE Multimed. **18**, 62–67 (2011)
13. Bao, Y., Wu, H., Zhang, T., Ramli, A.A., Liu, X.: Shooting a moving target: motion-prediction-based transmission for 360-degree videos. In: Joshi, J., Karypis, G., Liu, L., Hu, X., Ak, R., Xia, Y., Xu, W., Sato, A.H., Rachuri, S., Ungar, L., Yu, P.S., Govindaraju, R., Suzumura, T. (eds.) 2016 IEEE International Conference on Big Data (Big Data), pp. 1161–1170. IEEE, New York (2016)
14. Bao, Y., Wu, H., Ramli, A.A., Wang, B., Liu, X.: Viewing 360 degree videos: motion prediction and bandwidth optimization. In: 2016 IEEE 24th International Conference on Network Protocols (ICNP) (2016)
15. Qian, F., Ji, L., Han, B., Gopalakrishnan, V.: Optimizing 360 video delivery over cellular networks. In: Proceedings of the 5th Workshop on All Things Cellular Operations, Applications and Challenges – ATC 2016, pp. 1–6. ACM Press, New York (2016)
16. Hosseini, M., Swaminathan, V.: Adaptive 360 VR video streaming: divide and conquer (2016)
17. Niamut, O.A., Thomas, E., D'Acunto, L., Concolato, C., Denoual, F., Lim, S.Y.: MPEG DASH SRD. In: Proceedings of the 7th International Conference on Multimedia Systems – MMSys 2016, pp. 1–8. ACM Press, New York (2016)

18. Corbillon, X., Simon, G., Devlic, A., Chakareski, J.: Viewport-adaptive navigable 360-degree video delivery. In: 2017 IEEE International Conference on Communications (ICC), pp. 1–7. IEEE (2017)
19. Kuzyakov, E., Pio, D.: Next-generation video encoding techniques for 360 video and VR. https://code.facebook.com/posts/1126354007399553/next-generation-video-encoding-techniques-for-360-video-and-vr/
20. Kuzyakov, E.: End-to-end optimizations for dynamic streaming. https://code.facebook.com/posts/637561796428084/end-to-end-optimizations-for-dynamic-streaming
21. Kuzyakov, E., Chen, S., Peng, R.: Enhancing high-resolution 360 streaming with view prediction. https://code.facebook.com/posts/118926451990297/enhancing-high-resolution-360-streaming-with-view-prediction/
22. Bibiloni, T., Oliver, A., del Molino, J.: Automatic collection of user behavior in 360° multimedia. Multimed. Tools Appl. 1–18 (2017). https://doi.org/10.1007/s11042-017-5510-3
23. Experience API (xAPI) - Video Vocabulary. http://xapi.vocab.pub/datasets/video/
24. The Registry. https://registry.tincanapi.com/

IDTV Interaction Techniques and Accessibility

Proposal of a Tangible Interface to Enhance Seniors' TV Experience: UX Evaluation of SIX

Ana Patrícia Oliveira$^{(\boxtimes)}$ ⓘ, Mário Vairinhos ⓘ, and Óscar Mealha ⓘ

University of Aveiro – DeCA, Aveiro, Portugal
{apoliveira,mariov,oem}@ua.pt

Abstract. The computational innovations of recent years have enabled the emergence of a new technological paradigm that allows everyday objects to integrate new usages with the reception and transmission of information. These objects are now referred to as smart objects, because they augment the user interaction by connecting to the Internet and embedding electronic sensors. This new use of objects in daily life presents several conceptual, technological, economic and social challenges.

This paper presents and describes the SIX, an artifact with a tangible interface with the shape of a cube to select TV channels. One of the aims of the SIX is to abolish seniors' difficulties when they interact with a TV remote control, namely selecting channels. In order to understand the expectations and needs of seniors while they are using the SIX, an empirical study was performed, which characterized the affordance of the SIX. The methodological approach for the evaluation was based on User Experience (UX) and Usability tests. This empirical study was intended to improve the SIX in terms of its handling (ergonomics), interaction and appearance (aesthetics), meeting the needs of its target audience. This paper will also report on the empirical study's method and results' analysis and discussion.

Keywords: Tangible interface · Television · Internet of Things · Cube
TV remote · Evaluation · UX · Seniors

1 Introduction

Computing and electronics are increasingly common in people's lives and the interaction with physical objects, with affordance in place, becomes so intuitive that their materiality remains in the background and the attention is first directed into the task achievement.

The TV remote control is a common electronic device that is part of everyday life. However, the experience of using it is not always intuitive and efficient, it usually lacks affordance. Basic tasks as switching channels can become confusing and difficult for many people, mostly seniors, since its motricity is, sometimes, compromised (trembling hands and having imprecise movements). In addition to that, seniors usually suffer from visual impairing that makes it hard for them to see the small labels and symbols on the buttons of TV remotes, which are also small with little space between them [1–4].

© Springer International Publishing AG, part of Springer Nature 2018
M. J. Abásolo et al. (Eds.): jAUTI 2017, CCIS 813, pp. 135–149, 2018.
https://doi.org/10.1007/978-3-319-90170-1_10

The challenge of the present work is to design and create a tangible interface for changing channels that is easy to perceive, use and manipulate, which meets the needs of the largest group of users and adapts to the purposes of Universal Design.

The desired level of technology mediation is as close as possible to the interaction with the real world, in the way that the tangible interface operating mode should not impose restrictions or ruptures on everyday activities.

It is intended that the use of a tangible interface offers an inclusion opportunity to all those users that, from the point of view of accessibility, are somehow excluded from the electronic and/or digital world due to the impossibility of interacting physically and cognitively with conventional interfaces such as the TV remote control.

2   Theoretical Background

The direct manipulation of physical objects does not require, usually, a new type of learning for the user. According to the behavioral approach of cognitive psychology, people develop throughout their lives, in a process of adaptation to the environment, the understanding to act in the physical world that surrounds them. It is in this perspective that the concept of affordance arises, originally introduced by Gibson [5]. According to the author "the affordances of the environment are what it offers the animal, what it provides or furnishes, either for good or ill".

Later, this concept was further developed by Norman [6] who understood that its application to the development of interfaces in the daily artifacts has the advantage of releasing the subject from the interaction with a set of technical conventions.

More recently, the notion of affordance, which in its core includes the physical properties of real world objects, has been appropriated and applied in the field of graphical interfaces. Norman, realizing that the concept of affordance could not designate the visual metaphors present in a two-dimensional graphics system, proposed the term of "perceived affordance" to differentiate this scenario. "[…] in design, we care much more about what the user perceives than what is actually true. […] where one deals with real, physical objects, there can be both real and perceived affordances, and the two need not be the same" [7].

In this context, people interact with everyday objects in the same way they interact with another human being, through gestures, voice or eye movement. The objects and, in a broader way, houses, buildings and cities are extended with new features, uses and services through sensors and wireless connections that are present in our daily lives in different places and contexts. This is the paradigm of the Internet of Things, a term which is used to describe the connectivity between objects (things) and technology. The Internet of Things Council [8] defines it "as the seamless flow between the BAN (body area network): wearables, LAN (local area network): smart home, WAN (wide area network): connected car, and VWAN (very wide area network): the smart city. Key to this flow is having control of the data."

The idea of a physical object as an interface for a digital system explores the conceptual advantages of the Tangible User Interfaces (TUI) interaction paradigm. TUI "act as physical manifestations of computation, allowing us to interact directly with the portion that is made tangible – the tip of the iceberg" [9]. The integration of the physical and digital world will be highlighted by the advances in the Physics and Chemistry areas that will make intelligent and dynamic materials available.

3   Related Work

Regarding the interaction paradigm through objects with TV, namely cubes, there are no available options on the market that exclusively interact with TV. Currently, the available cube-shaped devices assume the role of remote controls for smart houses, controlling several appliances at the same time. Three products are described below:

(a) The Xiaomi Mi Cube [10] is a small cube with a 45 mm edge that contains a gyro-scope and an accelerometer. The Mi Cube controls smart home devices through six pre-programmed movements (push, shake, double-tap, rotate, flip 90° and flip 180°). For example, with the Mi Cube, it is possible to change the home light intensity by flipping the cube 180° and turning the TV off with a simple double-tap on the cube. This cube only interacts with the Xiaomi ecosystem.

(b) The "Family of the Arts" company created the Cube [11], a tangible interface that intends to be a universal controller for devices in smart homes. Cube fits in the palm of a hand and can be placed on any surface. To turn Cube on, it is necessary tap it on a surface, so that each side reveals its function through a backlit icon. For example, if user wants to listen to music, Cube must be flipped with the face with this function on top. It is not yet possible to purchase Cube, as it is still in the prototype stage.

(c) Orvibo Magic Cube [12] is a smart home control center that can work with almost all infrared appliances (95%) on the market, such as TV, air conditioner, DVD player, electric fan, etc. This cube controls home appliances with one smartphone and allows creating a personal smart home control network. Magic Cube works like a bridge between a WiFi and IR signal. For example, in a hot day, it is possible to switch on the air conditioning and the electric fan, remotely, by a smartphone.

Concerning scientific works with cubes as tangible interfaces for TV, there are two prototypes that should be mentioned in the context of the present study:

(a) Block et al. in 2004 [13] created an input device for changing TV channels in a more playful way. This prototype embeds gravity sensors and wireless communi-cation capabilities. The software developed specifically for it includes a 3D graph-ical interface where the cube is virtually represented on screen and it has a TV channel stream rendered on each of its faces. The motion on screen of this virtual cube is connected to the physical motion performed by the user on the real tangible artifact.

(b) The ARemote [14] is a cube that selects television channels in a predefined large list through simple rotational and translational gestures. A camera is used to visu-alize the movements of the cube and the cube's software interprets them and controls the selection of channels. The ARemote uses three interaction techniques: (a) circular scrolling strategy, in which the list can be scrolled with rotational gestures and the item can be selected by performing a quick vertical gesture; (b) circular scrolling with crossing strategy, with which the user can select the channel by crossing its graphical representation border with the mouse pointer and (c) crossing strategy, where the items are displayed in an alphabetical grid around the screen and the user must move the mouse pointer to the desired item and cross its border.

The SIX, described in this paper, differs from these solutions because on the one hand, the products available on the market are targeted to an audience with a high digital literacy, the so-called power users, on the other hand, the presented scientific works are more technically and conceptually complex prototypes than the SIX.

Thus, the SIX is designed for a specific audience (seniors) who have special needs when handling a conventional TV remote control, due to motricity problems, trembling hands and vision problems, being a technologically and conceptually simple and accessible solution. One of the aims of the SIX is the resolution of seniors' difficulties when they interact with a TV remote control, namely switching channels and while doing so, it improves their quality of life.

4   Accessibility and TV

Promoting the inclusion of people with special needs is an increasing concern that has supported changes in social and technological terms. Nevertheless, there is still a need to create more and better mechanisms and tools to ensure an effective participation of these citizens in several domains of society.

In order to promote the development of strategies and methodologies to accommodate a wide range of users' skills, capabilities, needs and preferences, it is important to emphasize the Universal Design approach. The Centre for Excellence in Universal Design (CEUD) defines Universal Design as "the design and composition of an environment so that it can be accessed, understood and used to the greatest extent possible by all people regardless of their age, size, ability or disability" [15].

For many people with special needs, the accessibility to information and communication technologies is determined by how easy it is to work with the system interface. The emphasis on human diversity is the most distinctive element of the Accessibility area. Systems should not be designed without considering the characteristics, needs, interests, preferences and behaviors of users [16].

However, the exclusive focus on Accessibility as a measurable item is not the most appropriated strategy to help users with special needs. According to Nielsen [17], a Usability perspective must be adopted in order to support these users, when they perform critical tasks. It is important to note that Usability is not a one-dimensional property. The International Organization for Standardization (ISO) described usability by a combination of factors including effectiveness: accuracy and completeness with which users achieve specified goals; efficiency: resources expended in relation to the accuracy and completeness with which users achieve goals; and satisfaction: freedom from discomfort and positive attitudes towards the use of the product [18].

Regarding the Television area, there are studies that suggest the application of principles and standards of accessibility and usability to solve the problems of users with special needs in the access and use of television devices and interfaces.

One of these studies was carried out by Springett and Griffiths [19], who suggested the application of WC3 accessibility principles in the design of the interactive services provided by Digital Television. In this line, Chorianopoulos [20] also proposed a set of interface design principles for iTV applications, based on the Human-Computer Interaction discipline. Finally, Oliveira et al. [21] conceptualized, prototyped and validated an iTV service adapted specifically to users with visual impairment to promote their digital inclusion.

The SIX responds to the principles of Universal Design, since it can accommodate a broad spectrum of users and usage contexts, not necessarily restricted to the seniors' limitations. Despite seniors can take benefit from this artifact, people with special needs, such as blind or partially sighted people and people with physical disabilities in the upper limbs can also take advantage from the SIX. Other potential users are young children (specifically between 2 and 3 years old) since they do not understand numbers and their fine motor skills are still in development. Moreover, people without special needs can identify utility in the SIX, because it simplify motor coordination actions and allows the interaction of the users with the TV to become more natural and intuitive, while promoting the sensorial recognition and manipulation of the object.

5   SIX

5.1   Description and User Scenario

The SIX intends to be a tangible interface for changing TV channels. The cube name (SIX), simply referring the number 6 and invoking the six degrees of freedom (6dof) in which an object can move in a three-dimensional space.

The cube (Fig. 1) consists of six faces in which one corresponds to the standby function and the remaining five to different channels customized by the user. The electronic parts of the cube are integrated inside it.

Fig. 1. The SIX with personalized paper labels (standby symbol and channels logos)

The user activates the desired channel on TV by manipulating the cube and putting the corresponding face turned upwards. The object is also physically customizable by the user who can write the channel name or draw on each of its faces through paper labels. Other materials can be used to wrap around the cube, such as rubber, plastic or padded fabric. For example, the cube's faces can be embossed with the numbers 1 to 6 in rubber or plastic, helping visual impaired seniors to identify each face.

Therefore, instead of associating buttons with numbers to TV channels, the user can move the cube and this action results in a channel change (causal reasoning), which makes their interaction experience more natural.

Here is one example of user scenario about the details of how this cube system might be interpreted, experienced and used:

Mrs. Robinson is a senior who has vision problems and trembling hands. As a hobby, Mrs. Robinson likes to watch television but she has difficulty in using the remote control. Her son, recognizing his mother's limitation, decides to offer her the SIX Cube. He only had to add his mother's four favorite TV channels (free-to-air) to the cube's faces. He printed the channels logo in a bigger size, almost covering the entirety of the cube's face, so his mother can recognize better to which channel a face corresponds. Now, Mrs. Robinson can enjoy zapping and choose easily the program of her choice.

5.2   Conceptual Model and System Architecture

A cube is a solid object with a strong psychological affordance, directing the subject's action to very standardized handling scenarios dominated by its six faces. In idle state, a cube has the natural tendency to immobilize on a single face, allowing the face turned upwards to be more prominent. When a cube is handled, through an exploratory movement, the attention is directed to one face at a time. These aspects give to a cube the true quality of a "state machine", in which only one of the elements is active.

The tangible interface of the SIX is in line with the TUI's approach that is based on the Model-View-Controller (MVC) pattern, in which the physical object is simultaneously an input (control) and an output (representation) of the system [22]. Like an abacus, the cube is both a representation and a control system, as it allows the user to send information of the wanted channel and to know what channel is displayed on TV by observing the top face of the cube. This double feature creates the feeling in the user that the concept of channel is incorporated in the cube.

In a conventional TV remote control, the physical buttons assume the role of the system input. The user is aware of the system status (selected channel, volume, etc.) through representations (outputs) that are not directly related to the TV remote control. Thus, the user does not know which channel is active from the simple observation of the TV remote control, since this information is only available through external representations in the system, such as the channel logo or the set-top box (STB) display. Opposite to the SIX, the conventional TV remote control is based on the Model-Control-Representation (MCR) interaction, in which the user input and the corresponding output can diverge both spatially and temporally.

Inside the SIX, a microcontroller, through an Inertial Motion Unit (IMU), recognizes in real time its orientation in space and sends to the STB an HTTP GET request with the key code that corresponds to the function, depending on the face that is facing up. The chosen microcontroller was the Arduino mini 3.3v (UC1, Fig. 2), due to accessible programming and the existence of a miniaturized microcontroller model on a printed circuit board (PCI) with small size. The cube orientation detection is performed from the integrated data of a gyroscope and an accelerometer that are sensitive to the 3 axes (UC2, Fig. 2). The chosen unit was the IMU 6DOF – Ultra Thin that includes the gyroscope and the accelerometer in a single PCI of small dimensions. In the version presented here only the data from the accelerometer was considered, however, the integration of the gyroscope will create, in the future, analogue inputs (as volume control or image contrast) by the precise rotation of the cube. The system incorporates a WiFi Module ESP8266 that allows sending HTTP GET requests to the STB through a serial protocol based on AT[1] commands (UC3, Fig. 2).

Fig. 2. Unit controllers of the SIX

The SIX was developed for the Portuguese IPTV service MEO[2], but can easily be adapted to other TV services and STB.

6   Evaluation of SIX

6.1   Methodological Approach

The empirical study was conducted at the "Patronato de Nossa Senhora de Fátima de Vilar" in Aveiro, Portugal with 15 senior users who attend the Adult Day Care Centre. This study aims to understand the expectations and needs of senior participants when

---

[1] The AT is an ATTENTION command and is used as a prefix to other parameters in a string.
[2] MEO is a trademark of the Altice Group.

using and interacting with a new domestic object: the SIX. The contribution of each participant is essential to improve the SIX in terms of its handling (ergonomics), inter-action and appearance (aesthetics).

Before the study was carried out, 3D printing of two more cubes was performed (Fig. 3), each one with different characteristics (a larger yellow and a smaller white one, both having rounded corners) in order to perceive the preference of seniors between the three cubes with distinct features regarding color, shape, weight, size and faces identi-fication. The only cube with electronic functions that was used by the seniors for direct interaction with the TV was the yellow one, since it better accommodated the electronic components and the power supply unit. The remaining cubes (white cube with numbers and transparent cube with logos) had a placeholder that emulated the electronics weight. This way, there were no differences in weight between the cubes other than the physical structures of each one of them.

Fig. 3. The three tested cubes, highlighting the two cubes that are 3D printed (arrows). (Color figure online)

Prior to the beginning of the evaluation, the participants were informed about all aspects of the study (nature, duration, methods and aims). In addition, the participants' anonymity was ensured through the agreement and signing of an informed consent document.

The methodological approach of the study was based on the combination of User Experience (UX) and Usability tests. With the aim of identifying and understanding better the way users describe UX, a set of evaluation methods is used along the empirical study, being them the semi-structured pre-interview, the think aloud protocol, a standard questionnaire (Likert-type scale) and the semi-structured post-interview [23].

The methodological approach was composed of the following stages:

Stage 0: Explanation of the study and presentation of the informed consent to participants.

Stage 1: Pre-test interview with the aim of promoting empathy with the researcher and understanding the participants' use of TV, their expectations using a TV remote control and their difficulties and needs when watching television.

Stage 2: Direct manipulation of the SIX by the participants, with video and audio recording regarding the experience, behavior and the think-aloud protocol. The researcher supports the participant if and only when he/she requests help. In addition to providing support, the researcher takes notes during the test. This activity is intended to understand, in a context of real and autonomous use by each participant, the usage model of the SIX in a direct interaction with the TV, considering the channels preprogrammed on the SIX.

Stage 3: Final and brief interview to understand each participants' thoughts on the use of the SIX and the classification of statements about the interaction with the SIX (Likert-type scale), by filling a form with a scale of semantic valuation, from 1 to 5, in which 1 means nothing; 2 means little; 3 means neutral; 4 means reasonable and 5 means a lot. This stage is intended to understand how participants evaluate various attributes related to their interaction with SIX (utility, satisfaction, ease of use, autonomy, what they like and do not like), which are included in each statement/question.

Stage 4: Presentation of three different cubes to understand the preferences of the participants regarding the shape, color, weight, size and identification of the faces of each cube.

Based on the study of Winckler et al. [23], we have adopted and included a set of six UX dimensions, as reported in the article, on the stages of the methodological approach so that the results reflect the assessments of UX. We have adapted the empirical approach of Winckler et al. in the sense that our methodology does not analyze the UX dimensions from the results, but we include these dimensions on the inquiry process of the stages, as follow:

Dimension of Visual and aesthetic experience – understanding the visual preferences of the participants regarding the three cubes (Stage 4).

Dimension of Emotion – understanding users' perceptions and emotions when using the SIX and what they like or do not like in the artifact (Stage 2 and 3).

Dimension of Stimulation – enthusing seniors to new impressions or opportunities, asking them about their expectations about new methods to control the TV (Stage 1).

Dimension of Identification – understanding how participants manipulate the SIX (usage model) (Stage 2).

Dimension of Meaning and value – understanding which values and attributes the product can satisfy (Stage 3).

Dimension of Social relatedness – understanding if watching TV for seniors is a social experience and if the SIX enables a wider, faster and more frequent interaction with the TV, being it a social medium (Stage 1 and 3).

6.2 Results' Analysis and Discussion

Stage 1: The study had a sample of 15 participants, 11 women and 4 men, aged between 76 and 99 years. Therefore, the mean age of the participants is 86 years.

All seniors watch television (a mean of 2 h a day) and everyone likes it too, with the TV being one of their main activities in daily life. In fact, seniors seem to be social included and connected to the world by TV.

Most participants (12 seniors) use the TV remote autonomously, while the remaining 3 seniors need help from other people in handling all tasks on the remote control.

9 seniors of the 12 participants, who handle the remote control, use the numbered keys to change channels, 2 seniors use the directional keys (up and down) and 1 senior uses both methods. In fact, seniors associate the television channels with specific numbers and most of the time they identify the channel not by its name, but by the number that is represented on the remote control/TV screen.

As for the number of channels they watch, the majority of participants (11 seniors) watch up to 4 television channels, 2 seniors watch between 5 and 6 channels and the remaining 2 state to see more than 10 different channels. In this way, the cubes' six faces can embody the favorite channels of the majority of seniors.

Regarding the expectations of the seniors about controlling the TV, the majority (12 seniors) could not answer the question "What other method would you like to use to change TV channels and control the sound volume?". Only 3 seniors pointed out methods that were categorized as voice recognition, gesture recognition and a method without the need of pressing keys (not knowing how to explain which) (Table 1). Most seniors seem to adapt to their own limitations (both physical and digital literacy) and resign to what is required from them in response to solutions of various situations in their daily lives, often because they consider themselves to be very old (+80 years) and those issues for them "are no longer something to concern".

Table 1. Categories of the alternative methods for controlling the TV

Category	Frequency	Participant statement
Voice recognition	1	"I would like to talk to the television and it would do what I said"
Gesture recognition	1	"I would like to indicate the channel number with my fingers and the television would change the channel"
A method without the use of keys	1	"The one that would give me less work, if I would not have to press any keys, the better"

Stage 2: All seniors quickly realized what SIX's main functionality was, taking a mean of 28 s to select a channel for the first time. Some comments while using SIX were: "Oh, this is perfect for me, I am so lazy, just turn and go."; "I can use this instead of the remote, right?"; "For people who do not move their hands very well, like my sister, this is very good" (Fig. 4).

Fig. 4. A senior participant using the SIX and watching the result of the interaction on TV

Another important aspect to note is that seniors, who did not use autonomously the TV remote, were able to select a TV channel without the help of others by using SIX. Thus, we believe that the autonomy of seniors can be clearly enhanced by the use of this artifact.

Stage 3: Some statements were formulated as a consequence of the seniors' evaluation with the scale of values previously explained. The statements were the following: (i) "SIX is a useful object." (attribute of utility); (ii) "I was satisfied with the use of the SIX." (attribute of satisfaction); (iii) "SIX is an easy to use object" (ease of use attribute); (iv) "I do not need the help of others when using SIX." (attribute of autonomy). Regarding the results of the value scale, every senior evaluated the attributes of utility, satisfaction, ease of use and autonomy with 4 or 5 values. Thus, the mean value of each attribute was as follows (Fig. 5): (i) Utility: 4,53; (ii) Satisfaction: 4,73; (iii) Ease of use: 4,73 and (iv) Autonomy: 4,47. These results reveal evidence of a very positive experience of the seniors, since the mean value of all the attributes is very close to the maximum. Thus, we believe that the experience of using the SIX has met the majority of the expectations, desires and needs of the participants.

After categorizing the given answers by the seniors about what they liked in the SIX, the channel switching functionality is what 1/3 of seniors liked best. Another category with the highest number of occurrences is "Everything", in which seniors say they like everything about the SIX (Table 2). All the seniors pointed out something they like on the SIX, which demonstrates a generalized satisfaction with the object.

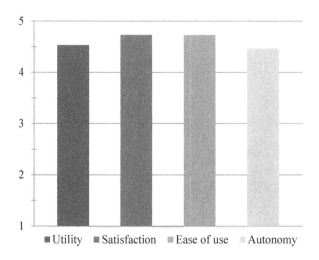

Fig. 5. Mean values of the attributes of usability, satisfaction, ease of use and autonomy

Table 2. Categories about what seniors like in the SIX

Category	Frequency	Participant statement
Functionality	5	"I like how I change the channel"; "Switching channels"; "I really liked the functionality of it"
Everything	3	"I like everything"
Appearance	2	"I like the color"; "It's beautiful"
Concept	2	"It's a good idea"; "It's practical, I like the idea"
Speed	1	"It switches channels quickly"
Utility	1	"It's useful for people with physical disabilities"
Novelty	1	"It is modern"

Regarding what seniors do not like about the SIX, almost half of the seniors said there was nothing they did not like. On the other hand, the size (pointed by 6 seniors) and weight (pointed by 2 seniors) of the SIX, was what they dislike (Table 3). Seniors preferred the SIX to be smaller and lighter because it would be more practical and more comfortable for them.

Table 3. Categories about what seniors do not like in the SIX

Category	Frequency	Participant statement
Nothing	7	"Nothing"
Size	6	"It's too big"; "I don't like the size"; "The size, it's big"; "The size and the weight"
Weight	2	"The cube is heavy"; "The size and the weight"
Do not know	1	"I don't know"

All seniors said that with the SIX they change channels more easily than with a TV remote. This reflects the unanimous acceptance of this new artifact by the seniors, in addition to revealing the potential of replacing the usual TV remote with the SIX.

Stage 4: When asked which of the three cubes was preferred, in almost all the characteristics, the choice of the seniors pointed to the white cube (the smallest cube and with numbers on the faces), only in the color preference did the seniors select another cube, in this case the yellow version. The unanimity of the choices is also quite evident. Thus, (i) as to color, most seniors (10) selected the yellow cube; (ii) as to form, the majority (10) chose the white cube; (iii) concerning weight, all seniors selected the white cube; (iv) regarding size, all seniors also preferred the white one; (v) as to identification of faces, the majority (10) also chose the white cube (which had numbers on the faces); (vi) concerning the easiest cube to manipulate, the preference of all seniors was on the white cube; and finally (vii) the cube they like best, the white cube was likewise selected by the seniors.

In this way, it is verified that seniors prefer a cube with a more vibrant color than a neutral one and having a rounded shape in the corners. In addition, the cube should not be heavy and should be relatively small, fitting in the palm of the hand in order to be handled more comfortably. Each of the cube's faces should identify the desired channels through numbers instead of logos, since the seniors have difficulties in identifying and associating logos with the television channels.

7   Final Remarks and Future Work

TUI devices emphasize the direct physical manipulation because due to their property of being touchable, they produce interfaces that take advantage of the human senses and of the kinesthetic involvement of the body in space. The Six Cube is within these assumptions combining accessibility and affordance, enabling seniors to select TV channels through a tangible interface that is easy to perceive, use and manipulate, improving their quality of life and sense of belonging to the domestic ecosystem.

Regarding future work, the authors will improve the responsive mobile interface (that already exists) for the SIX configuration, where we can introduce the connection details to the Wi-Fi network and the desired channels for each of SIX's face. In addition, the physical structure and ergonomics of the SIX will be improved, taking into account the results obtained in the evaluation of the SIX by seniors in this study. New features will be added to the SIX, such as the rotation to control the TV sound volume or the rotation to do zapping by theme (an opportunity of reaching new audiences). Finally, a new UX and Usability evaluation cycle will be performed and published with these new features.

Acknowledgments. The authors would like to acknowledge AlticeLabs@UA for funding this project and Patronato de Nossa Senhora de Fátima de Vilar (Aveiro) for their partnership in the evaluation of the SIX.

References

1. Bernhaupt, R., Desnos, A., Pirker, M., Schwaiger, D.: TV interaction beyond the button press. In: Abascal, J., Barbosa, S., Fetter, M., Gross, T., Palanque, P., Winckler, M. (eds.) INTERACT 2015. LNCS, vol. 9297, pp. 412–419. Springer, Cham (2015). https://doi.org/10.1007/978-3-319-22668-2_31

2. Epelde, G., Valencia, X., Carrasco, E., Posada, J., Abascal, J., Diaz-Orueta, U., Zinnikus, I., Husodo-Schulz, C.: Providing universally accessible interactive services through TV sets: implementation and validation with elderly users. Multimed. Tools Appl. **67**(2), 497–528 (2013). https://doi.org/10.1007/s11042-011-0949-0

3. Bobeth, J., Schmehl, S., Kruijff, E., Deutsch, S., Tscheligi, M.: Evaluating performance and acceptance of older adults using freehand gestures for TV menu control. In: Proceedings of the 10th European Conference on Interactive TV and Video (EuroITV 2012), pp. 35–44. ACM, New York (2012). https://doi.org/10.1145/2325616.2325625

4. Lessiter, J., Freeman, J., Miotto, A., Ferrari, E.: A comparative study of remote controls for digital TV receivers. In: Tscheligi, M., Obrist, M., Lugmayr, A. (eds.) EuroITV 2008. LNCS, vol. 5066, pp. 318–322. Springer, Heidelberg (2008). https://doi.org/10.1007/978-3-540-69478-6_42

5. Gibson, J.: The Ecological Approach to Visual Perception. HM Publications, Boston (1979)

6. Norman, D.: The Psychology of Everyday Things. Basic Books, New York (1988)

7. Norman, D.: Affordances and Design. The Nielsen Norman Group (2004). http://www.jnd.org/dn.mss/affordances_and.html

8. IOT Council, What is the Internet of Things? http://www.theinternetofthings.eu/what-is-the-internet-of-things. Accessed 19 July 2017

9. Ishii, H., Lakatos, D., Bonanni, L., Labrune, J.B.: Radical atoms: beyond tangible bits, toward transformable materials. Interactions **19**(1), 38–51 (2012). https://doi.org/10.1145/2065327.2065337

10. Xiaomi Global Community, Xiaomi Mi Smart Home Cube White. https://xiaomi-mi.com/mi-smart-home/xiaomi-mi-smart-home-cube-white. Accessed 10 July 2017

11. Family of the Arts, Cube. http://www.familyofthearts.com. Accessed 10 July 2017

12. Orvibo, Orvibo Magic Cube Wifi Remote Control. http://www.orvibo.com/en/product/46.html. Accessed 10 July 2017

13. Block, F., Schmidt, A., Villar, N., Gellersen, H.W.: Towards a playful user interface for home entertainment systems. In: Markopoulos, P., Eggen, B., Aarts, E., Crowley, J.L. (eds.) EUSAI 2004. LNCS, vol. 3295, pp. 207–217. Springer, Heidelberg (2004). https://doi.org/10.1007/978-3-540-30473-9_20

14. Tahir, M., Bailly, G., Lecolinet, E.: ARemote: a tangible interface for selecting TV channels. In: Proceedings of the 17th International Conference on Artificial Reality and Telexistence, pp. 298–299. IEEE (2007). https://doi.org/10.1109/icat.2007.11

15. The Centre for Excellence in Universal Design (CEUD), What is Universal Design. http://universaldesign.ie/What-is-Universal-Design/. Accessed 19 July 2017

16. Klironomos, I., Abascal, J.: An Introduction to the Key Issues Relating to Accessible User Interfaces, Cardiac Project, EU (2010). http://www.cardiac-eu.org/user_interfaces/key.htm

17. Nielsen, J.: Accessibility Is Not Enough, Nielsen Norman Group (2005). http://www.nngroup.com/articles/accessibility-is-not-enough/

18. International Organization for Standardization (ISO): Guidance on Usability, ISO 9241-11: 1998, ISO (1998)

19. Springett, M.V., Griffiths, R.N.: Accessibility of interactive television for users with low vision: learning from the web. In: Cesar, P., Chorianopoulos, K., Jensen, J.F. (eds.) EuroITV 2007. LNCS, vol. 4471, pp. 76–85. Springer, Heidelberg (2007). https://doi.org/10.1007/978-3-540-72559-6_9

20. Chorianopoulos, K.: User interface design principles for interactive television applications. Int. J. Hum.-Comput. Interact. **24**(6), 556–573 (2008). https://doi.org/10.1080/10447310802205750

21. Oliveira, R., Abreu, J., Almeida, M.: Promoting interactive television (iTV) accessibility: an adapted service for users with visual impairments. Univers. Access Inf. Soc. **16**(3), 533–544 (2017). https://doi.org/10.1007/s10209-016-0482-z

22. Ishii, H.: Tangible bits: beyond pixels. In: Proceedings of the 2nd International Conference on Tangible and Embedded Interaction, pp. xv–xxv. ACM, New York (2008). https://doi.org/10.1145/1347390.1347392

23. Winckler, M., Bernhaupt, R., Bach, C.: Identification of UX dimensions for incident reporting systems with mobile applications in urban contexts: a longitudinal study. Cogn. Technol. Work **18**(4), 673–694 (2016). https://doi.org/10.1007/s10111-016-0383-1

Audio Description of Television Programs:
A Voluntary Production Approach

Rita Oliveira , Jorge Ferraz de Abreu , and Ana Margarida Almeida

University of Aveiro - DigiMedia, Aveiro, Portugal
{ritaoliveira,jfa,marga}@ua.pt

Abstract. Audio description (AD) is an audiovisual translation technique targeted to visually impaired people enabling them the full access of visual content. This technique can be applied in several contexts, as is the case of Television, where a professional storyteller describes the visual scenes not perceptible by viewers with blindness and low vision, based on a pre-produced script made by a screenwriter. In this way, the production of AD is a costly and complex process, involving different professionals and procedures. Besides that, many countries, like Portugal, do not respect the minimum obligations mandated by the law related to the use of audio description in television programs. Despite this scenario, the current television eco-system provides possibilities to enhance this technique, leveraging the number of audio described TV content for people with visual impairment. In order to change this situation, we intend to develop a platform that supports AD production for television programs based on a voluntary model.

In this context, the paper aims to describe the platform, pointing out its functional requirements from a comparative study between the professional process of AD production and the voluntary approach to be developed.

Keywords: Accessibility · Television · Visual impairment · Audio description
Volunteering

1 Introduction

Audiovisual translation is commonly used in the television context, especially to help the interpretation of foreign content, using techniques such as subtitling and dubbing. When the contents are in native language other techniques, like voice-over and description, also support a specific kind of audiovisual translation. In these techniques, the management of verbal and nonverbal components of the narrative are required [1], demanding human intervention. The role of these techniques in the development of accessible TV contents is of major importance, because they enable its access to people with special needs. In the specific case of viewers with visual impairment, they benefit from audio description (AD).

Audio description is a media feature designed for visually impaired people to enable, via audio, the access to visual content, such as TV programs, in which a storyteller describes scenes that are not perceptible by these users [1]. The 'RTP1' (the public

Portuguese TV station) is the only one in Portugal that broadcasts regularly some of its programs with AD [2], although other Portuguese stations are also required by law to broadcast programs with AD [3]. Viewers with visual impairment can access AD through two ways: by radio or Digital Terrestrial Television (DTT). These options are only compatible with the DTT platform, excluding customers of pay-tv services (the TV platform more used in Portugal). Besides that, most of the time, audio description (for television and other contexts) is performed by qualified professionals through specific technical resources, which makes it financially expensive. Therefore, the creation of a model of volunteering to perform audio descriptions of TV programs clearly becomes advantageous.

In this context, this paper is based on a project that suggests a new approach for the creation of TV audio descriptions that is supported in the recording of real time audio descriptions made by volunteers who do not need to have technical skills to perform the process. On the one hand, the project intends to offer more AD for TV through the development of a cross-platform application for the creation of audio descriptions by volunteers and, on the other hand, it aims to change the way audio description is accessed by viewers with visual impairment through the development of an Interactive Television (iTV) application accessible to this public. In this paper, the platform to be developed is described and its functional requirements are identified from a comparative study between the professional process of AD production and the voluntary approach.

In the next sections, the state of the art related to this field of research is presented and the platform for the creation of audio descriptions is described. After that, the methodology that was used to conduct the study is explained, pointing out the results obtained. The paper closes with the final comments and the work to be done in the next phase of this study.

2   Related Work

In Portugal, the current situation concerning the relationship between users with visual impairments and television demands more effort in this research field, since there is a significant number of people with this type of impairment who do not entirely benefit from the capabilities of the current TV paradigm, such as audio description. According to the 2011 Portuguese Census, 9.3% of the population over 5 years old (about 921,000 people) is visually impaired, 97% of them (about 893,000) have great difficult in seeing and the remaining 3% (about 28,000) are blind [4]. Besides that, Portuguese viewers with visual impairment can only follow some series of RTP1 (the public Portuguese TV station) with audio description. This AD is accessible through an outdated system - the medium wave of Antena1 (the Portuguese public Radio station). The TV program is broadcasted via the free to air TV network and the audio description is simultaneously broadcasted via radio. More recently, through the Digital Terrestrial Television (DTT), the RTP1 audio description is broadcasted in a secondary audio channel but this setup is still inconsistent [2].

The international scenario on the audio description is quite different from Portugal. For instance, in the UK the broadcasters have a legal obligation to provide at least 10%

of its programming through audio description [5] and in USA, the local stations of the 60 zones of the country with greater use of Television are obliged to broadcast about 4 h a week of programs with audio description [6].

However, the Portuguese academia being worried with this situation has performed significant efforts to counteract it. Neves [7] is a precursor of several projects that encourage the use of audio description in several domains. Oliveira et al. [8] has some work in the field of interactive television, suggesting an adapted system to visually impaired users supporting access to audio description. In Spain, the 'AudescMobile' mobile application was created allowing the access to AD of several types of audio-visual productions, using audio fingerprinting (analysis of a sound excerpt recorded by the application) [9]. The WhatsCine app [10], also created in Spain, allows the access of audio description, subtitling and sign language in television and movie theatres. In Brazil, there are projects related to the promotion of audio description; for example, Campos [11] suggests a mechanism based on semantic web application for the automatic creation of audio description for movies and Domingues et al. [12] proposes an automatic system to create audio descriptions. In the United States of America there is a free and experimental tool developed as part of an academic research that allows adding audio descriptions on YouTube videos [13]. The audio descriptions can only be created and accessed through the 'YouDescribe' web tool.

Concerning the volunteer model to provide inclusive services, there are several European initiatives that take advantage of it for the creation of audiobooks [14–16], audio description book illustrations [15] or audio newspapers [17] and for the supply of geographical information [18] and social initiatives [19].

In Europe, there are also more extensive audiovisual translation projects, such as the 'HBB4ALL' [20] that aim to promote a wider availability of accessible media aids to all viewers with special needs (like audio description, subtitles and sign language). The project aims to make a cross-platform production and distribution of accessibility features more cost-efficient and more flexible and easier to use, benefiting users and also broadcasters and media producers.

3   Real-Time Audio Description Supported in Volunteering

In this section, the new approach for the creation of audio descriptions by volunteers is described.

The real-time audio description is supported on a volunteering approach that has as main target relatives of visual impaired viewers for the creation of audio descriptions. Usually, these persons have a predisposition for description because they regularly help their visually impaired relatives during daily activities, such as watching TV, reporting what is happening on the screen. So, the advantages of this model are the reduction of costs in the production of audio description and consequently the greater offer that it generates.

In a starting study related with this technique (previously performed by the authors of this paper) it was possible to find that volunteers were satisfied with the procedure used to create AD and visually impaired users felt that this type of AD assisted them

[21]. It is worth to say that as these new approaches demand a preprocessing phase, they are especially relevant for non-linear TV programs, for instance those available from the video-on-demand (VOD) service or the Catch-up TV service of Pay-Tv providers.

The concept for the real-time and voluntary approach will be supported in a cross-platform solution (web and mobile) for iTV and will be sustained in the following workflow (Fig. 1): (1) recording of the segments of real-time audio description to be carried out by the volunteers synchronously with the television content (the platform will recognize the favorable moments for inserting the AD segments); (2) uploading of the resulting audio file into an audio descriptions repository (after the upload, it is intended that the community itself evaluate the audio descriptions in a gamification model, through, for example, assignment of points); (3) providing the audio description through an iTV application (usually a catch-up TV program or other non-linear one). It is also foreseen to provide the possibility of selecting the audio description by various criteria (e.g. name of the author or rating).

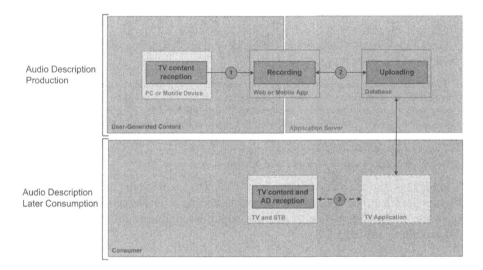

Fig. 1. Workflow of the voluntary approach for AD creation

4   Study of the Functional Requirements of the Platform of Voluntary AD

Before starting the identification of the functional requirements of the platform of voluntary audio descriptions, it was necessary to deeply understand the concept and creation process of audio description. After this analysis, the authors were enabled to proceed to the comparison between the professional process of AD production and the voluntary approach. From this comparison, the authors identified and defined the functional requirements of the platform.

4.1   Concept and Creation Process of AD

Audio description is an audiovisual translation technique specially designed and developed for people with visual impairment and is susceptible of application in various spaces and contexts such as TV programs, cinematographic content, performing arts, DVD's, museum contents as well as cultural spaces. The descriptions of dynamic visual elements of movies, TV programs and performing arts should be inserted into the pauses of the original soundtrack of the production. It is important to avoid AD over audio that is essential to comprehend the narrative, but it can happen when is necessary to provide crucial and imperative information. Besides that, it is also important to leave pauses without AD when is appropriate to support the ambience [22]. In this sense, audio description only makes sense in combination with the original sounds, music and dialogues. For dynamic narratives, AD can be recorded (e.g. movies and TV programs), or it can be performed live (e.g. performing arts). In the case of movies and TV programs, a storyteller does the description of the scenes or images that are not noticeable by the visually impaired viewers and that description is broadcasted usually when there are no dialogues.

The United States Government deliberates audio description as an accessibility standard and describes it as follows [23]:

> *"Narration added to the soundtrack to describe important visual details that cannot be understood from the main soundtrack alone. Audio description is a means to inform individuals who are blind or who have low vision about visual content essential for comprehension. Audio description of video provides information about actions, characters, scene changes, on-screen text, and other visual content. Audio description supplements the regular audio track of a program. Audio description is usually added during existing pauses in dialogue. Audio description is also called "video description" and "descriptive narration".".*

In Fig. 2 is shown a scene of the movie 'The Interviewer' where the main character (Thomas) is silent but his expression reveals that he is displeased with something because he is pursing his lips. A possible audio description of this scene could be: "Thomas purses his lips…".

Fig. 2. A scene of 'The Interviewer' and its corresponding audio description [24]

In this context, the audio description production for movies and TV programs follows several specific sequential steps. Based on relevant references in this field [7, 25–27], the authors of the paper identify four main steps, which are described below:

1. Study and Script Creation: A professional audio descriptor studies the audiovisual piece to be described and produces a script with the text to be narrated, which follows specific guidelines. The most common guideline is inserting audio description excerpts into pauses in dialogues (if it is possible).
2. Tests and Adjustments: After the script conclusion, the audio descriptor should test the descriptions positions in the previously chosen locations. In addition, time adjustments and/or vocabulary replacement are also made.
3. Recording: At this stage, the audio descriptor comes into a studio with the recording director and a technician to perform the recording of the script descriptions.
4. Synchronization/Mixing: The recorded audio file is edited and associated to the original soundtrack of the movie or program in a new audio file, or in a specific audio channel.

4.2   Comparison Table

The comparison table was prepared taking into account the four main steps to produce audio description for TV: Study and Script Creation; Tests and Adjustments; Recording; and Synchronization/Mixing. To analyze these four steps and establish a correlation between the proposed voluntary approach and professional AD, different procedures within each step were identified. The Table 1 compares professional AD and the proposed voluntary approach according to the AD creation process for TV.

With the analysis of the comparison table, it was possible to verify that the creation process of the proposed voluntary approach is quite different from the production method of professional audio description.

Regarding the first step 'Study and Script Creation', the voluntary approach differs from the professional method in the form of elaborating AD, because the voluntary approach has no script and AD creation is only based on the direct understanding of the narrative by the volunteer. Concerning the second step 'Tests and Adjustments', the main difference between the two methods is the fact that in the professional AD, the audio describer can make tests and changes in the AD segments, but in the voluntary approach, the volunteer has no physical support to make any kind of changes. Considering the 'Recording' step, in the professional AD, the audio describer records audio description in a meticulous way, supported by the script and with the help of other professionals. On the other hand, in the voluntary approach, the volunteer records audio description in real-time and singlehanded. Regarding the last step 'Synchronization and Mixing', the main difference between the two methods is the fact that in the voluntary approach the volunteer has no access to the final audio file, contrary to what happens in the professional method, since the audio describer has the possibility to make a final edition in the created AD file. Besides that, in the professional AD, the audio describer has no responsibilities in the association of the AD file to the TV program; however, in the voluntary approach, the volunteer should perform the AD file uploading to make the association.

Table 1. Comparison between professional AD and the proposed voluntary approach

AD production steps for TV	Procedures	Professional AD	Voluntary approach
1. Study and script creation	Movie study	The audio describer has the possibility to view and study the entire movie	The volunteer has the possibility to view the entire movie before creating AD if he wants
	Script writing	The audio describer elaborates a script that will guide him during AD	The volunteer creates AD based on his direct understanding of the narrative
	Pauses identification	The audio describer identifies the pauses to adjust AD content to them	The volunteer can identify the pauses only while he is creating AD
2. Tests and adjustments	Position testing	The audio describer verifies if the position of AD segments is correct	The volunteer can verify if the AD segment overlaps with the original soundtrack only after recording
	Time adjustments	The audio describer can adjust AD times according to tests	n/a
	Text adjustments	The audio describer can adjust AD texts according to tests	n/a
3. Recording	recording	The audio describer records the AD in a studio	The volunteer records the AD in real-time and in a domestic environment
	Recording control	The audio describer has the help of the studio director and a technician	The volunteer records the AD without assistance
4. Synchronization and mixing	Final edition	The audio describer makes a final edition on the AD file	The volunteer can repeat the recording of each AD segments if he wants
	Association to TV program	The AD association to TV program is made by a technician	The volunteer makes the AD association to TV program through web uploading

4.3 Identification of the Functional Requirements

The findings obtained from the analysis of the comparison table enabled the identification of the functional requirements of the platform that will support the voluntary approach for AD creation. These requirements were categorize based on the procedures involved in the production of audio description for TV and are following described.

- Movie study:

The volunteer has access to the moments that should be audio described and, if he wants, he has the possibility to view the entire movie before creating AD. So, the platform should provide the user with the possibility of watching the preceding TV content of these moments and also the entire movie. The duration of the precedence should be variable depending on the user's level of knowledge about the movie. Besides that, the user should be informed about the number of segments to be described and the segment where the user is.

- Script writing:

As the volunteer has no access to any script, he creates AD segments based on his direct understanding of the narrative. Thus, the platform should include tips on how to create helpful audio descriptions in a specific section.

- Pauses identification:

As the platform automatically identifies the favorable moments for inserting the AD segments, the volunteer can recognize the pauses only while he is creating AD. In this way, the platform should inform the user about the recommended duration of the AD segments. Besides that, the platform should provide the user with the possibility of skipping the segments that he thinks do not need AD.

- Position testing:

As mentioned in the previous point, the platform automatically identifies the moments for inserting AD. Therefore, the volunteer can verify if the AD segment overlaps with the original soundtrack only after recording. For this reason, the platform should inform the user about when he should start and end the AD segments recording.

- Time and Text adjustments:

The volunteer cannot directly adjust AD times, because this recognition is done by the platform. The volunteer cannot also adjust AD texts, because there is no script. The platform should provide the user with the possibility to record again the AD segment.

- Recording:

The volunteer records the AD segments in real-time and in a domestic environment. Thus, the platform should clearly inform the user when is necessary to start and end an AD segment recording, for example with a strategy of counting down. The user should also be informed during the process that the recording is being made.

- Recording control:

As the volunteer records the AD singlehanded, the strategy of include tips on how to create helpful audio descriptions should be used not only in a specific section but also during the recording process without disturbing the user.

- Final edition:

The volunteer does not have access to the AD file and cannot make a final edition of the file. However, the user should have the possibility to view the final result and repeat any of the segments.

- Association to TV program

The volunteer makes the AD association to TV program through web upload. Before making the association, the user should be informed about how many segments he recorded and how many segments he skipped. Besides that, when the upload is complete, the user should be notified.

5   Conclusions and Future Work

The info-inclusion of people with disabilities is becoming a reality. However, it is necessary to study and develop more services and tools that allow all citizens to participate actively and autonomously in society. This problem is particularly critical in usage scenarios involving mass media like Television (TV), specially taking in consideration its audiovisual format (which involves image, sound and text) that are not perceptible by many of viewers with special needs, such as visually impaired persons.

The comparative study described in this paper, allowed us to identify and understand the functional requirements of the platform for the AD creation. Besides that, the researchers can confirm that the proposed voluntary AD production approach is a suitable solution for the accessibility to audiovisual content for visually impaired viewers, because it could be an alternative to the method of professional AD production.

From the presented results, we are now able to extend this research with an additional study about the functional requirements that brought up with the study presented in this paper. The authors are conducting a study with a low-fidelity prototype, which is being tested with potential volunteers, enabling the identification and definition of the final functionalities inherent to the proposed model. In the next phase, we will prototype the components of the proposed model, in order to test and validate the voluntary audio description technique with volunteers and consumers.

Acknowledgements. Authors are grateful to FCT and FSE for the financial support to this research (ref. SFRH/BPD/112129/2015) under the 3rd European community support framework.

References

1. Chaume, F.: The turn of audiovisual translation: new audiences and new technologies. Transl. Spaces **2**(1), 105–123 (2013). https://doi.org/10.1075/ts.2.06cha
2. Rádio Televisão Portuguesa (RTP): RTP Acessibilidades (2018). http://www.rtp.pt/wportal/acessibilidades/audiodescricao.php. Accessed 05 Jan 2018
3. Autoridade Nacional de Comunicações (ANACOM): Television Law - 8/2011 (2011). http://www.anacom.pt/render.jsp?contentId=1105582#.VdYYplVVikp. Accessed 05 Jan 2018

4. Instituto Nacional de Estatística (INE): Censos - Resultados definitivos: Portugal - 2011 (2012). http://censos.ine.pt/xportal/xmain?xpid=CENSOS&xpgid=ine_censos_publicacao_det&contexto=pu&PUBLICACOESpub_boui=73212469&PUBLICACOESmodo=2&selTab=tab1&pcensos=61969554. Accessed 05 Jan 2018
5. Office of Communications (Ofcom), Audio Description makes the story clearer (2018). https://www.ofcom.org.uk/tv-radio-and-on-demand/information-for-industry/guidance/programme-guidance. Accessed 05 Jan 2018
6. The Audio Description Project (ADP): Top 60 Markets Which Must Provide Audio/Video Description (2018). http://www.acb.org/adp/tvfcctop60.html. Accessed 05 Jan 2018
7. Neves, J.: Imagens que se Ouvem – Guia de Audiodescrição, Instituto Politécnico de Leiria, Leiria (2011)
8. Oliveira, R., Abreu, J., Almeida, M.: Promoting interactive television (iTV) accessibility: an adapted service for users with visual impairments. Univers. Access Inf. Soc. 16(3), 533–544 (2017). https://doi.org/10.1007/s10209-016-0482-z
9. Organización Nacional de Ciegos Españoles (ONCE): Audesc Mobile: la audiodescripción en nuestra mano (2014). http://cidat.once.es/home.cfm?id=1516&nivel=2. Accessed 05 Jan 2018
10. Whatscine: Accesibilidad audiovisual en cines y television (2016). http://www.whatscine.es/. Accessed 05 Jan 2018
11. Campos, V., Araújo, T., Filho, G: CineAD: Um Sistema de Geração Automática de Roteiros de Audiodescrição. In: Simpósio Brasileiro de Sistemas Multimídia e Web (WebMedia) - IX Workshop de Teses e Dissertações (WTD) (2014). http://www.lbd.dcc.ufmg.br/colecoes/wtdwebmedia/2014/001.pdf
12. Domingues, L., et al.: GT-AaaS 2.0 - Acessibilidade como um Serviço com Foco em Pessoas com Deficiência Visual. In: 17º Workshop RNP (2016). http://wrnp.rnp.br/sites/wrnp2016/files/wrnp16_lamina_gtaaas_edit_v3.pdf
13. YouDescribe: A free accessibility tool for adding audio description to YouTube videos (2018). http://youdescribe.org/. Accessed 05 Jan 2018
14. Librivox: Acoustical liberation of books in the public domain (2018). https://librivox.org/. Accessed 05 Jan 2018
15. Projeto de Leitura Inclusiva Partilhada (PLIP): KITS PLIP (2018). http://plip.ipleiria.pt/dinamizacao. Accessed 05 Jan 2018
16. Biblioteca Nacional de Portugal (BNP): Leitura para Deficientes Visuais – Recursos áudio (2018). http://www.bnportugal.pt/index.php?option=com_content&view=article&id=121&Itemid=155&lang=pt. Accessed 05 Jan 2018
17. National Talking Newspapers and Magazines (NTNM): About Our Service (2018). http://www.tnauk.org.uk/index.html. Accessed 05 Jan 2018
18. Parker, C., May, A., Mitchell, V., Burrows, A.: Capturing volunteered information for inclusive service design: potential benefits and challenges. Des. J. 16(2), 198–218 (2013). https://doi.org/10.2752/175630613X13584367984947
19. Paredes, H., Fernandes, H., Sousa, A., Fortes, R., Koch, F., Filipe, V., Barroso, J.: CanIHelp: a platform for inclusive collaboration. In: Antona, M., Stephanidis, C. (eds.) UAHCI 2015, Part II. LNCS, vol. 9176, pp. 474–483. Springer, Cham (2015). https://doi.org/10.1007/978-3-319-20681-3_45
20. HBB4ALL: Hybrid Broadcast Broadband For All - Connected TV Accessibility (2016). http://www.hbb4all.eu/. Accessed 05 Jan 2018
21. Oliveira, R., Abreu, J., Almeida, M.: Audio description in interactive television (iTV): proposal of a collaborative and voluntary approach. Procedia Comput. Sci. 100, 935–940 (2016). https://doi.org/10.1016/j.procs.2016.09.252

22. DCMP: Description Key (2018). http://descriptionkey.org/how_to_describe.html. Accessed 05 Jan 2018
23. Federal Register: Information and Communication Technology (ICT) Standards and Guidelines (2017). https://www.federalregister.gov/documents/2017/01/18/2017-00395/information-and-communication-technology-ict-standards-and-guidelines. Accessed 05 Jan 2018
24. Bus Stop Youtube: The Interviewer - Captions & Audio Description (2015). https://www.youtube.com/watch?v=rgRv4bSdLdU. Accessed 05 Jan 2018
25. Remael, A., Reviers, N., Vercauteren, G.: Introduction: basic audio description concepts. In: Remael, A., Reviers, N., Vercauteren, G. (eds.) Pictures Painted in Words: ADLAB Audio Description Guidelines. Edizioni Università di Trieste, Trieste (2015). http://www.adlabproject.eu/Docs/adlab%20book/index.html
26. Fryer, L.: An Introduction to Audio Description: A practical guide. Routledge, New York (2016)
27. Greening, J., Rai, S., Leen, P.: A Comparative Study of Audio Description Guidelines Prevalent in Different Countries. Media and Culture Department, Royal National Institute of Blind People, London (2010). http://audiodescription.co.uk/uploads/general/RNIB._AD_standards.pdf

An Open and Extensible Platform
for Machine Translation of Spoken
Languages into Sign Languages

Rostand Costa[(✉)] [iD], Tiago Maritan [iD], Renan Soares, Vinicius Veríssimo,
Suanny Vieira, Alexandre Santos, Manuella Aschoff, and Guido Lemos

Digital Video Applications Lab - LAVID, Federal University of Paraíba - UFPB,
João Pessoa, Brazil
{rostand,maritan,renan,vinicius,suanny,alexandre,
manuella,guido}@lavid.ufpb.br

Abstract. The purpose of this paper is to investigate the feasibility of offering
a multilingual platform for text-to-sign translation, i.e., a solution where a
machine translates digital contents in several spoken languages to several sign
languages in scenarios such as Digital TV, Web and Cinema. This solution called
OpenSigns, is an open platform that has several common components for generic
functionalities, initially originated from the **Suíte VLibras**, including the creation
and manipulation of 3D animation models, and interchangeable mechanisms
specific for each sign language, such as a text-to-gloss machine translation engine,
a sign dictionary for each sign language, among others. Our motivation is that the
concentration of efforts and resources around a single solution could provide some
state-of-the-art improvement, such as a standard solution for the industry and a
greater functional flexibility for common components. In addition, we could also
share techniques and heuristics between the translation mechanisms, reducing the
effort to make a new sign language available on the platform, which may further
enhance digital inclusion and accessibility, especially for poorest countries.

Keywords: Digital video · Online video · Accessibility · Sign language
Machine translation

1 Introduction

In Brazil, according to the 2010 census of the Brazilian Institute of Geography and
Statistics (IBGE), there are approximately 9.7 million Brazilians with some type of
hearing loss, representing 5.1% of its population [9]. The World Health Organization
estimates that approximately 360 million people worldwide have some level of hearing
loss [13].

This relevant part of the population faces several challenges in accessing information, usually made available through written or spoken language. The main problem is
that most deaf people spend several years in school, but are not proficiency in reading
and writing the spoken language of their country. One of the possible explanations is
the fact that these languages are based on sounds [16].

A study carried out in 2005 with 7 to 20 years old Dutch deaf persons found that only 25% of them had a reading capacity equal or greater than a 9-year-old child without disability [18].

One of the reasons for this difficulty is that the deaf communicate naturally through sign languages (SL), and spoken languages are only a "second language". Each SL is a natural language, with its own lexicon and grammar, developed by each deaf community over time, just as each hearing community developed its spoken language. Thus, there is no unique SL. Although there are many similarities between all these languages, each country usually has its own, some even more than one - by 2013, there were already over 135 sign languages cataloged around the world [1].

In order to allow adequate access, one solution is to translate/interpret spoken contents into the associated SL. However, considering the volume and dynamism of information in some environments and platforms, such as on the Web, performing this task using human interpreters is not viable, considering the high volume of content that is added daily on the Internet. In the context of Digital TV, the support for sign languages is generally limited to a window with a human sign language interpreter, which is displayed overlaying the video program. This solution has high operational costs for generation and production of the contents (cameras, studio, staff, among others), needs full-time human interpreters, which ends up restricting its use to a small portion of the programming. To address this question pragmatically, one of the most promising approaches today is the use of tools for machine translation of a spoken language into a SL.

Proportionately to the number of SL, there are also numerous parallel initiatives to build machine translation tools for these SLs, usually focused on the scope of a single language/country, some even competing with each other. Most of these text-to-sign machine translation tools, although conducted completely independently in their respective countries, have similarities in approach, scope, and architecture. In general, the basic functionalities are present in some form in most of them. Steps such as extraction of the text to be translated from audio and subtitles, generation of the sign language video, incorporation of the sign language videos into the original videos (e.g., on Digital TV), spelling and rendering of glosses by plugins and mobile applications, etc. There are also similarities in the structure and behavior of components, such as APIs and backends of communication, translation and control, etc.

The main points of variation are usually the specific mechanism of translation and the dictionary of signs of the language (visual representation of signs). For the latter and considering the use of avatars, the modeling process of visual represention is similar (e.g., a set of animations) and usually depends on the allocation of financial and human resources, regardless of the technology used.

To reduce this problem, the objective of this paper is to propose an open, comprehensive and extensible platform for *text-to-sign* translation in various usage scenarios and countries, including Digital TV. In the proposed platform, the common components share generic functionalities, including the creation and manipulation of the dictionaries.

Only the translation mechanism and the dictionary itself are interchangeable, being specific to each SL. To accelerate the development, we used the Suíte VLibras[1] as a basis.

Our motivation is the concentration of efforts and resources around an unique solution that can be able to provide cutting edge gains, such as the definition of patterns for the industry standard and greater functional flexibility for the common components, and also allow advances in the state-of-the-art, such as sharing techniques and heuristics among translation mechanisms.

A single standardized platform with centralized processing of multiple sign languages can also serve as a catalyst for more advanced translation services, such as incorporating text-to-text conversion. In this sense, available translation mechanisms between spoken languages can be integrated to allow Deaf in Brazil or Spain to understand, in Brazilian Sign Language (LIBRAS) or Spanish Sign Language (LSE), respectively, a text in English, for example.

Another contribution is to leverage the emergence of a common core rulebased translator that can be extended/adapted to meet new languages and regionalisms. Reducing the effort to make a new SL available may further enhance digital inclusion and accessibility, in technologies such as Digital TV, Web and Cinema, especially in the poorest countries.

The remainder of the paper is organized as follows. Section 2 lists some of the machine translation tools available in the scientific literature. Section 3 presents the proposal generic platform for machine translation of spoken language to sign language. Section 4 presents a prototype of the proposed platform as proof of concept. This prototype accepts input texts in any spoken language and translates into three target sign languages. Section 5 finally brings our conclusion and final remarks.

2 Machine Translation Platforms for Sign Languages

Machine translation systems for sign language are generally divided into three main classes: Rule-Based Machine Translation (RBMT), Statistical Machine Translation (SMT) and Example-Based Machine Translation (EBMT) [17]. One important challenges of such systems is to ensure that the content available to Deaf has the same consistency and quality of the original content, allowing the adequate understanding of the message.

Considering these systems may be a viable alternative to minimize the marginalization of Deaf, especially through digital inclusion, several researches have been developed around the world focusing on the development and offering of operational platforms for machine translation of spoken languages into SL [2, 4].

---

[1] The **Suíte VLIBRAS** is the result of a partnership between – removed for blind review, and consists of a set of tools (text, audio and video) for the Brazilian Sign Language (LIBRAS), making TVs, computers, mobile devices and Web platforms accessible to deaf. Currently, VLibras is used in several governmental and private sites, among them the main sites of the Brazilian government (brasil.gov.br), Chamber of Deputies (camara.leg.br) and the Federal Senate (senado.leg.br). Further information can be obtained from http://www.vlibras.gov.br.

In Brazil there are at least four platforms available for machine translation of Brazilian Portuguese digital contents into LIBRAS: **Suíte VLibras** [7, 8], **HandTalk** [3], **ProDeaf** [5] e **Rybená** [6].

The **Suíte VLibras** consists of a set of open source computational tools, responsible for machine translating digital content into Brazilian Portuguese for LIBRAS, making the information available on computers, TVs, mobile devices and Internet portals accessible to Deaf. The VLibras main components are:

- *VLibras-Plugin*: a browser extension that allows the translation of any selected text to LIBRAS;
- *VLibras-Mobile*: VLibras clients for mobile devices (both iOS and Android);
- *VLibras-Desktop*: is a Tool used to translate into sign language any marked text taken from applications running on personal computers;
- *VLibras-Video*: is a portal that allows translation to LIBRAS of audio tracks or subtitles associated with videos;
- *LibrasTV:* an adaption of VLibras for the Brazilian Digital TV system.

3   OpenSigns: A Proposal of a Multilingual Machine Translation Platform

It is a consensus that machine translation does not match the quality of a human interpreter in capturing and transmitting all the nuances of a message. However, the use of glosses and animation can be a complementary and practical solution, especially when human interpreters are not available or are not feasible.

In this sense, the main contribution of our work was the transformation of a complete platform of automatic translation from Brazilian Portuguese (written or spoken) to LIBRAS, called VLibras, into an extensible platform, called OpenSigns.

The new platform can be expanded with the addition of new text-to-gloss translators with support for other pairs of spoken languages and sign languages. In the restructuring of the platform, an additional step of automatic text-to-text translation was also included in order to extend the scope of each specific text-to-gloss translator to other input languages.

During our study, we identified that a number of features of the original platform (VLibras) were agnostic regarding input and output languages and possibly applicable to other contexts directly. Thus, among the technological tools already available in the generic platform (OpenSigns), we can mention:

- **Plug-ins** for many popular browsers that allow texts on web pages to be captured, submitted to a remote text-to-gloss translator and the resulting glosses rendered by an avatar (Fig. 1).
- **TV applications** for the most popular platforms that allow the presentation of sign language contexts available on Digital TV signal.
- **Mobile applications** for the two most popular platforms that allow the translation and rendering of signals from an input text, also using a remote text-to-gloss translator (Fig. 2).

Fig. 1. VLibras Plugin

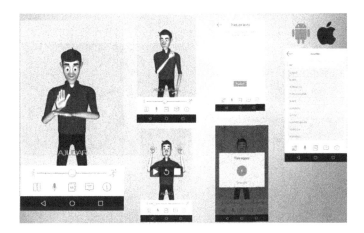

Fig. 2. VLibras Mobile

- **Desktop applications** for major operating systems that allow content from multiple sources on the user's computer to be translated and rendered offline (Fig. 3).
- **Extraction mechanisms** of texts from audio and videos for later translation text-to-gloss.
- A **web portal** for on-demand text translation, performed by an internal text-to-gloss translator.
- A **web portal** for video translation resulting in a new video with a signal language window synchronized with the original audio (Fig. 4).

Fig. 3. VLibras Desktop

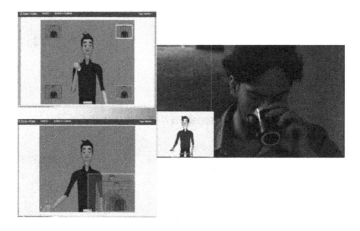

Fig. 4. VLibras Video

An integrated set of tools like this for machine translation using avatars is not easy to build and we believe that few initiatives in the world have such reach and penetration, with a dictionary with more than 13,500 LIBRAS 3D modeled signs. With the effort of generalization practiced in this work, this framework is available to be extended and used in other countries and languages.

The main effort to include the treatment of a new sign language is the creation of the 3D sign language dictionary and the addition of the associated text-to-gloss translator. The text-to-gloss translation components have been carefully isolated on the new platform so they can be easily retrofitted and/or replaced.

In this sense, the focus of this research was to validate previously three aspects of the new platform:

- If the new text-to-text translation step, which converts any spoken language into the reference spoken language of the desired sign language, inserts too much noise into the quality of the generated gloss;
- If the process of incorporating new text-to-gloss translators is feasible and simplified;
- If the process of setting up a new text-to-gloss translator (for example, ASL) using the generic internal translator with morphological, semantic and syntactic treatment is feasible.

The experiments and comparison of the obtained results were concentrated in the result of the gloss obtained automatically with respect to the glosses produced by human interpreters. They considered results in previous works, including validated in real experiments done with users.

4 Proof of Concept: Text Translation in Any Language for LIBRAS, LSE or ASL

4.1 Prototype Architecture

We started with an initial assessment that good part of the **Suíte VLibras** components had generic features that could be shared among several sign languages with minor changes. The main changes needed were aimed at making the components that access the translation services "agnostic", ie, independent of the input and output languages. In addition, we also focused on enabling the solution to support multiple machine translation engines and multiple sign dictionaries.

Figure 5 illustrates the architecture of the *VLibras Suite* [8]. Initially, it only translated content from Brazilian Portuguese to Libras.

Figure 6 presents an adapted version of the original architecture, which includes support for multiple source and target languages. In the new architecture shown, the components highlighted in orange and red represent the points of variance and have been rebuilt to support multiple input and output languages.

The components in blue had their basic behavior maintained. The minor adjustments required are related to the generalization and internationalization of their interface.

4.2 Prototype Implementation

To develop a proof of concept of the proposal platform, initially, we developed a translator prototype able to translate texts into any spoken language of source into three target SLs: LIBRAS, LSE and ASL.

The text-to-text pre-translation module was created using the Google Cloud Translation API[2], to convert texts in any spoken language into Portuguese, Spanish or English depending on the target sign language.

---

[2] This API is able to identify the input language of a sentence and translate it automatically into a target spoken language (www.google.com/translate).

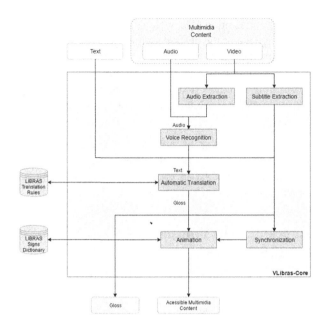

Fig. 5. Internal architecture of *VLibras*

Then, the text-to-gloss translation module was adapted to support the translation of sentences in Brazilian Portuguese (BP), English or Spanish for a sequence of glosses

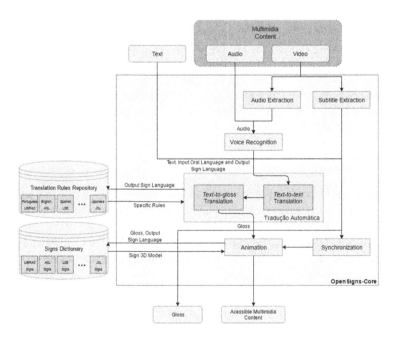

Fig. 6. Internal architecture of *OpenSigns* (Color figure online)

into LIBRAS, ASL or LSE respectively. The tokenization (i.e., the separation of words from each sentence) in English or Spanish languages was made specifically for each of them, taking into account their own structural characteristics.

We also adapted the process of generation of sentence syntax trees for English and Spanish new translation modules. Figure 7 bring one example of syntactic trees for the same sentence in BP, English and Spanish, respectively.

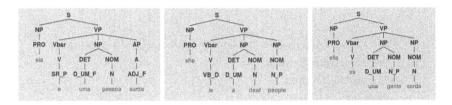

Fig. 7. Example of a sentence syntactic tree in BP, English and Spanish

We also have to make a mapping between the tags of the languages treated in the prototype and apply the syntactic description of the BP language. An excerpt from the crosstab that was created is illustrated in Fig. 8.

Grammatical Class	Portuguese (Aelius)	English (NLTK)	Spanish (Conll 2007)
PROPER NOUN	NPR	NNP	NP
PERSONAL PRONOUN	PRO	PRP	PP
POSSESSIVE PRONOUN	PRO$	PRO$	DP
INTERROGATIVE PRONOUN	-	-	PI
DEMONSTRATIVE PRONOUN	D	-	PD
PREPOSITION	P	IN	SP
VERB	VB	VB	V
MAIN VERB	-	-	VM
IMPERATIVE VERB	VB-I	-	-
PRESENT VERB	VB-P	VBP	-
PAST VERB	VB-D	VBD	-
CONDITIONAL FUTURE VERB	VB-R	-	-
DEFINITE ARTICLE	D	DT	DA
INDEFINITE ARTICLE	D-UM	DT	DI
DEMONSTRATIVE DETERMINE	DEM	-	DD
ADJECTIVE	ADJ	JJ	A
SUPERLATIVE ADJECTIVE	ADJ-S	JJS	-
ADVERB	ADV	RB	-
COORDINATING CONJUNCTION	CONJ	CC	CC
NUMERAL	NUM	CD	Z (digit) / DN (in words)

Fig. 8. Grammatical tags mapping between the source spoken languages

Thus, before the generation of the syntactic tree, the proper labels of English and Spanish are replaced by their grammatical equivalents in BP, if any. Such a temporary artifice used in the prototype may have some impacts on the generation of the syntactic tree of some sentences but does not make the translation process unfeasible.

The text-to-gloss translation is based on a set of grammatical rules specific to each language treated in the prototype. Such rules are aimed at the adequacy of the morphosyntactic divergences between the spoken language and the associated target sign language.

All rules, whether morphological or syntactic, are modeled in XML files. Basically, each rule contains information from which grammar class it is intended for and the action should be taken whether the rule applies to the sentence. The application of syntactic rules implies the updating of the syntactic tree in order to keep it consistent with the modifications made. Below we have an example of rule applied in prepositions (P) of BP:

```
                <rule name = "P"><!-- remove specific preposition -->
        <active>true</active>
        <count>1</count>
        <class>
            <title>P</title>
                <specific>x</specific>
                <action>remove</action>
        </class>
    </rule>
```

where

- *active* indicates that the rule is active, if its application is required;
- *count* is used for the next iteration with the sentence. In the case of BP prepositions, for example, only the current token will be evaluated. The next iteration should only advance one sentence token;
- *specific* is a specific action given to the need for translation into a target sign language. In the case presented, this action verifies whether the token is actually one of the prepositions of the spoken language;
- *action* is a generic action in case the outcome of the specific action is affirmative. The absence of a *specific* results in the execution of *action*. In the example, the prepositions are removed.

In this other example of treatment of verbs in the past, *newprop* specifies that the new token tag will be after the rule is applied. In that case, the part of the tag representing the verb tense (-D) will be removed, since the action made in this type of verb for the translation to LIBRAS is the conversion of the verb to the infinitive and the addition of a new tuple to the sentence containing the verb tense of the verb treated.

```
                <rule name = "VB-D"><!-- verb tense - past with advt-->
        <active>true</active>
        <count>1</count>
        <class>
            <title>VB-D</title>
                <specific>advt</specific>
                <action>change_vb</action>
            <newprop>VB</newprop>
        </class>
    </rule>
```

The two examples presented are morphological rules, but the syntactic rules follow the same pattern.

The adaptations made from BP to LIBRAS also use auxiliary dictionaries and algorithms for treatments of special plurals. In the morphological adaptations to English, auxiliary dictionaries are also used for the verification of some specific, as well as exclusive modules for verbal treatment and treatment of plurals, in both cases using algorithms based on WordNet[3]. In this first version of the prototype, in the translation from English to ASL and Spanish to LSE, only morphological adequacy is being done.

The post-processing step implemented in the *OpenSigns* prototype refines the translation in a specific way for each of the three SL. Some examples of steps performed in this step are: substitution of words or part of the sentence by a synonym, the substitution of numbers by numerals and identification of compound words, among others.

4.3 Experiments and Results

A set of tests was carried out to verify the feasibility of the proposal in the translation of sentences for ASL and LIBRAS.

The tests were performed using objective metrics WER (*Word Error Rate*) and BLEU (*Bilingual Evaluation Understudy*) [14], which are generally used to evaluate machine translation strategies [11, 15, 17]. According to Melo et al. [12], this type of computational test has the "purpose of evaluating machine translation systems with greater economy, speed and independence of languages than evaluations performed manually".

Initially, we performed a set of tests to evaluate the machine translation of sentences in English to LIBRAS. To perform this task, we used the same sentences of the corpus "Bosque" [10] used by Lima et al. [11] to evaluate the Suíte VLibras translation[4].

---

[3] https://wordnet.princeton.edu/wordnet/citing-wordnet/.
[4] In this test, the authors randomly selected 69 sentences and two LS interpreters generated a sequence of glosses in LIBRAS for each one. Then the VLibras translator was used to automatically generate a sequence of glosses of these same sentences and the values of the WER and BLEU metrics were calculated for the two scenarios.

In the tests with our prototype, these 69 sentences were initially translated from BP into English by an English specialist. Then, the OpenSigns prototype was used to machine translate these sentences in English for glosses in LIBRAS. Then, the WER and BLEU metrics, considering the precision in 1-grams (unigrams), 2-grams (bigrams), 3-grams (trigrams) and 4-grams, were recalculated for this sequence of glosses. The results can be seen in Table 1.

Table 1. BLEU and WER values for the 69 sentences of corpus Bosque

	VLibras [11]	OpenSigns
BLEU 1-grams	73.50%	56.80%
2-grams	61.20%	39.00%
3-grams	51.20%	27.70%
4-grams	43.00%	20.30%
WER	31.70%	55.00%

According to Table 1, the BLEU and WER values of VLibras were better than those of OpenSigns in all cases. This result was expected, since the sentences were translated using a single step of machine translation from BP to LIBRAS in VLibras. In the case of OpenSigns, on the other hand, the sentences were translated using two stages of translation (one from English to BP and the other from BP to LIBRAS), which explain the difference in the results.

However, we can observe that this difference of values was not so significant, considering that a new stage of translation was included. This difference was around 20% for all metrics. For the WER metric, VLibras obtained a value of 33%, whereas OpenSigns had a value of 55%, an average difference of 22%. In the BLEU metric, the difference was also in the range of 20%, for all n-grams.

It is also important to consider that despite having slightly lower values in translation metrics, OpenSigns has a great positive difference on VLibras: the possibility of a deaf user translating a text in a foreign language (possibly unknown to him) into his own sign language (e.g., LIBRAS), increasing the scope of inclusion of these users, allowing them to access texts in other spoken languages.

Table 2. BLEU and WER values for VLibras, OpenSigns and direct translation

	English-LIBRAS (OpenSigns)	BP-LIBRAS (VLibras) [11]	BP-LIBRAS (Direct Translation)
BLEU 1-grams	56.80%	73.50%	40.70%
2-grams	39.00%	61.20%	22.20%
3-grams	27.70%	51.20%	11.40%
4-grams	20.30%	43.00%	5.50%
WER	55.00%	31.70%	87.70%

In addition, the sentences in BP were also translated using a direct approach to gloss in LIBRAS, and WER and BLEU values were also calculated. Direct translation, as its

name implies, involves the literal translation of each term of the sentence to a correspondent in gloss, i.e. without processing, interpretation or analysis of the context. With
this, it is expected to contrast the translation made using VLibras, OpenSigns and direct
translation. Table 2 lists the BLEU and WER values for the three scenarios.

According to Table 2, we can observe there was a reduction in BLEU values, and
an increase in WER value, when the translation using the prototype is compared with
the translation generated by VLibras. As mentioned before, we expected a worse result
in OpenSigns due to the intermediate machine translation process text-to-text, which is
an inherent bias that can be reflected in the final result of the translation. The reduction
in BLEU values averaged 20% to 30%, which can in principle be considered an acceptable noise considering that there are two translation processes involved. However, it is
part of our future roadmap to conduct an experiment with deaf users to verify the level
of intelligibility of the translations obtained.

In any case, when we compare the machine translation of English to LIBRAS generated by the prototype with a direct translation strategy (from words in Portuguese for
glosses in LIBRAS), we can observe that there was an improvement in the results of the
BLEU and WER. This is an indication that the translation of sentences from English to
LIBRAS using the proposed approach has the potential to produce better results than a
direct translator of words to glosses. In other words, this result may point out that, even
containing an intermediate stage of translation from English to BP, the noise generated
in this process is not so high that it will not allow machine translation, since it had better
results than a direct translation from BP words to LIBRAS glosses.

Continuing the validation of the approach, we carried out a second set of tests with
the objective of evaluating the use of an additional translation stage between sign
languages, rather than a stage of intermediate translation between spoken languages.
For example, to translate English contents to LIBRAS, instead of translating from
English to Portuguese, and then translating to LIBRAS, we performed two step of translations: translation from English into ASL glosses, followed by a translation from ASL
to LIBRAS.

In this test, some English sentences (and their respective glosses in ASL) were
randomly selected from the *American Sign Language University* (ASLU)[5] site. After
the selection, a LIBRAS specialist with advanced knowledge in the English language,
translated all the sentences to a sequence of LIBRAS glosses.

The sentences in English were then submitted to the prototype and translated into
LIBRAS glosses. Then, the ASL glosses of these sentences were submitted to the prototype and translated into BP, and then to LIBRAS. The BLEU and WER values were
generated for the two scenarios based on the reference translation produced by the
LIBRAS specialist. The values of WER and BLEU obtained are shown in Table 3.

Analyzing the results, we can observe that the BLEU values are higher and the WER
value is lower in the first scenario, where the translation was made directly from the
sentences in LIBRAS. This result indicates that the translation of the sentence in a given
spoken language directly to the target SL, can offer better results than translation from
the gloss in another SL.

---

[5] www.lifeprint.com/asl101/index/sign-language-phrases.htm.

Table 3. BLEU and WER values for ASLU ASL sentences

	English-LIBRAS	ASL-LIBRAS
BLEU 1-grams	65.20%	47.80%
2-grams	42.60%	18.90%
3-grams	25.60%	0.00%
4-grams	14.20%	0.00%
WER	19.3%	28.0%

Afterwards, the sentences translated by the specialist were converted to a sequence of glosses in LIBRAS, where the VLibras and the prototype were again used to generate the sequence of glosses in LIBRAS from phrases and glosses randomly selected from the ASLU database[6]. With this, we can calculate the BLEU and WER values of the glosses in LIBRAS generated from the text in English and the glosses in ASL in order to analyze the best approach: direct translation of the sentence or translation from the gloss. Table 4 contains the percentage values of the two approaches.

Table 4. BLEU and WER values for the two approaches to translation

	Direct from English	Glosses in ASL
BLEU 1-grams	65.18%	47.80%
2-grams	42.58%	18.89%
3-grams	25.60%	0.00%
4-grams	14.18%	0.00%
WER	19.32%	28.02%

According to Table 4, we verified that the BLEU values are larger and the WER value is lower in the first approach, where the translation was performed directly from English to gloss in LIBRAS using the prototype. On the other hand, the second approach presented lower values in the BLEU and higher in the WER. In a first analysis, the direct translation of the sentence of a given language offered better result than from the gloss of another language.

5   Final Remarks

In this work, we present the results of a research whose objective is the development of a multilingual platform for "text-to-sign" machine translation, ie, a unique ecosystem that accepts several spoken languages as input and performs a machine translation for several output sign languages. The proposed platform is based on several common existing components, derivated from the **Suíte VLibras**, in which components supporting specific mechanisms of different sign languages have been added.

---

[6] http://www.lifeprint.com/asl101/index/sign-language-phrases.htm.

A prototype, based on an extension of **Suíte VLibras** was developed with the aim of verify that the basic concepts of the proposed platform are feasible. In this prototype, additional components have been implemented to support the translation of texts in any language for Libras and ASL.

In our conception, it is fundamental to stimulate the community of researchers and developers who work with translation support systems for sign language to collaborate. As we are distinct groups, in some cases with commercial interests and competing in the market for accessibility products, cooperation is only possible with the definition of standards for architecture and some system components. One of the components that is critical for the evolution of the results in the area is the dictionary. For us, the dictionary must be a resource shared by the different translation systems. This would imply in a more accelerated increase in the number of signs, quality and convergence in the use of signs. It is therefore vital to accelerate the definition and expansion of the sign languages themselves.

References

1. Deaf sign language on world. https://www.ethnologue.com/subgroups/deaf-signlanguage. Accessed 30 Nov 2016
2. Fundación hetah - herramientas tecnológicas para ayuda humanitaria. http://hetah.net. Accessed 29 Nov 2016
3. Hand Talkc. http://www.handtalk.me/. Accessed 25 June 2015
4. Learn Sign Language in a Playful Way with SiGame – The App. http://theartofservice.com/learn-sign-language-in-a-playful-way-with-sigamethe-app.html. Accessed 30 Nov 2016
5. ProDeaf. http://prodeaf.net/OQueE/. Accessed 25 June 2015
6. Rybená Web. http://www.rybena.com.br/site-rybena/conheca-o-rybena/web. Accessed 25 June 2015
7. Araújo, T.M.U.: Uma solução para geração automática de trilhas em língua brasileira de sinais em conteúdos multimídia (2012)
8. Araújo, T.M.U., Ferreira, F.L.S., et al.: An approach to generate and embed sign language video tracks into multimedia contents. Inf. Sci. **281**, 762–780 (2014)
9. IBGE: Population census 2010: General characteristics of the population, religion and people with disabilities. Technical report, Brazilian Institute of Geography and Statistics (2010). http://biblioteca.ibge.gov.br/visualizacao/periodicos/94/cd_2010_religiao_deficiencia.pdf. Accessed 20 Dec 2017
10. Freitas, C., Rocha, P., Bick, E.: Floresta sintá(c)tica: bigger, thicker and easier. In: Proceedings of the 8th International Conference on Computational Processing of the Portuguese Language, PROPOR 2008, Aveiro, Portugal, pp. 216–219 (2008)
11. Lima, M.A., Araújo, T.M., Oliveira, E.S.: Incorporation of syntactic-semantic aspects in a libras machine translation service to multimedia platforms. In: Proceedings of the 21st Brazilian Symposium on Multimedia and the Web, Webmedia 2015, pp. 133–140 (2015)
12. Melo, F.R., Matos, H.C.O., Dias, E.R.B.: Aplicação da métrica bleu para avaliação comparativa dos tradutores automáticos bing tradutor e google tradutor. E-scrita **5**(3), 33–45 (2014)
13. World Health Organization (WHO), et al.: Deafness and hearing loss, fact sheet n 300, updated February 2013

14. Papineni, K., Roukos, S., Ward, T., Zhu, W.: BLEU: a method for automatic evaluation of machine translation. In: Proceedings of the 40th Annual Meeting of the Association for Computational Linguistics, pp. 311–318 (2001)
15. San-segundo, R., Barra, R., et al.: Speech to sign language translation system for Spanish. Speech Commun. **50**(11), 1009–1020 (2008)
16. Stumpf, M.R.: Língua de sinais: escrita dos surdos na internet. In: V Congresso Ibero-Americano de Informática na Educação–RIBIE–Chile (2000)
17. Su, H.Y., Wu, C.H.: Improving structural statistical machine translation for sign language with small corpus using thematic role templates as translation memory. Trans. Audio Speech Lang. Proc. **17**(7), 1305–1315 (2009)
18. Wauters, L.N.: Reading comprehension in deaf children: the impact of the mode of acquisition of word meanings. EAC, Research Centre on Atypical Communication, Radboud University, Nijmegen (2005)

Author Index

Printed in the United States
By Bookmasters